Light in the Night
for
Living in the Day

LUD GOLZ

Dedication

To my four children

Greg, Debbie, Tammi and Jeff

my pride and joy.

Lud Golz

Acknowledgements

It is a joy when you get to the point of a project completed. It gives you a sense of accomplishment. When that project is a book you realize many have contributed toward it becoming a reality.

I will not attempt to list everyone who has had a part in the production of this book. My church made it possible for me to work on it over the last few years. My secretary, Valerie Aiken, helped at critical points. Some of my friends at the church read various drafts as I was refining the manuscript. Dave Lunka persisted in encouraging and supporting me in getting it into print. George Verwer kindly agreed to write the Foreword. Dr. Dennis Hensley helped me greatly at a writers retreat and then went over the manuscript with his keen editor's eye. Thank you all for your help.

My wife Muriel encouraged and supported me in whatever project I have tackled during our years of marriage and helped in this project as well. She deserves a lot of credit in its accomplishment.

Ultimately, my greatest help came from the enabling power of the Holy Spirit. My prayer is that He will use this book to inspire many in their life journey.

Lud Golz

Table of Contents

Foreword

Light has been a major word in my life. Even before my conversion I noticed how often it was referred to as I read the Gospel of John. On March 3, 1955 Jesus, the Light of the world, took over my life as by faith I received the gift of eternal life. After going to Mexico in the summer of 1957 I was led to start a ministry called, "Send the Light."

Around that time God led me to Moody Bible Institute and it was there I met Lud Golz. We started to meet regularly for prayer and I have been linked with Lud ever since.

I just preached to 20,000 people at a Campus Crusade event in Korea and I am writing this in the middle of the night. After a couple of hours of sleep, I woke up, picked up the manuscript of Lud's new book, "Light in the Night for Living in the Day." The message resonated with my passion and experience.

Many times God has met me in the night. Nights of prayer became a vital part of our movement which later in Europe became known as Operation Mobilization. During these nights of prayer God would put cities, peoples and nations on our hearts and we would later see breakthroughs in these nations in answer to those prayers.

Lud is a person who has walked with God for more than 50 years. I really believe we can be helped and inspired by what he shares with us in this book. As a young Christian, hungry for God's Word, I once stayed up late into the night and read the whole book of Acts. It was a significant milestone for me on my road to reality and discipleship as a Christian.

Today people often stay up late to watch Sports or a film, but how we need more Christians who will be up in the night to seek the Lord. This well thought-through book may help you do just that.

George Verwer

Introduction

"Even in darkness light dawns for the upright." (Psalm 112:4)

Many think that to get the most out of life you need to be a 24/7 kind of person. Yet, we all know we need anywhere from five to nine hours a day for sleep. If we don't get enough sleep it will affect the quality of our health and well being. God is different. He can and does function 24/7. He is not limited to working in our lives during our waking hours. He often uses the nighttime to reveal His special plans and to do much of His most significant work.

While I attended Wheaton College, then president Dr. V. Raymond Edman often said, "Never doubt in the dark what God told you in the light." It was an impact statement I've never forgotten. The implication of this statement was this: pray through the process of making a decision or determining God's will for your life. Once determined, don't doubt what God led you to conclude in the daylight. Even if your circumstances overwhelm you, and you feel unsure of yourself and confused, confidently implement your decision.

In recent years I've realized this truth could be stated another way. Namely, "Don't doubt in the daylight what God has told you in the darkness of night." Or light in the night for living in the day. At times, when facing a critical decision, I've been restless at night and found it difficult to sleep. Sometimes I have gotten up in the quietness of the night to talk to God and wait on Him. Not always, but often I would find that in the solitude and absence of distractions I would understand issues more clearly and see possibilities in sharper focus.

The more I thought about this, it caused me to remember from my Bible reading that God often confronted, enlightened and directed individuals in nighttime settings. Think of how God worked in Jacob's life. Jacob wrestled with the angel of the Lord all night, had his life transformed, and was given the new name of Israel. It was at night that the Exodus took place. Jesus won His greatest prayer victory in the garden of Gethsemane, at night. Paul received his Macedonian call at Troas during the night. This opened the door for the Gospel to spread into Europe. On and on individuals can be found who were given light in the night for living in the day.

I decided to read through the Bible and note all the recorded nighttime experiences. I was amazed to see how often God worked in the lives of individuals and even nations during the night. As I was working on this project I found in my other reading and in many conversations that this has been a common dynamic. People like Pascal, John Wesley, Billy Graham, Bill Bright, Charles Colson and many others have had powerful night time experiences that have profoundly changed and redirected their lives.

Maybe we hear better in the quietness of the night. Maybe we see the light better in contrast to the darkness around us. Maybe we turn to God more readily in the loneliness of the night. Maybe it's easier to surrender and take hold of God's hand to guide us when engulfed by the night's darkness.

Journey with me as I share with you some of the light I gained from observing how God at times works in lives, including my own, during the night.

Lud Golz
Novelty, Ohio

Chapter One

Guidance:
Where Do I Go from Here?

"You did not trust in the Lord your God, who went ahead of you on your journey, in fire by night and in a cloud by day, to search out places for you to camp and to show you the way you should go." (Deuteronomy 1:32-33)

As a pastor for more than 45 years I've had many distraught, confused people come to me for help. They've wanted me to give them answers that would get them through a crisis and, hopefully, out of the circumstances plaguing them. I'm often considered the answer-man. The challenge is to help them learn how to find the answer they need for themselves.

When I, personally, am faced with critical decisions, I usually go through the same analytical process I use to help others discern what they are facing. But when the decision is mine it's harder to be objective. I don't always see how the dots connect. With hindsight, however, I'm able to see how God has done some wonderful things to guide me, often pulling things together by giving me light in the night.

As I approached the age of 60 I began planning for the transition from being the founding Senior Pastor of my church to passing the baton of leadership to a successor. As I prayed about it, I kept getting the impression that I should be prepared to stay on staff after my successor was installed. With that in mind I thought it would be wise to talk to two of my staff members who had been with me for some time to see if they would fit in the Senior Pastor position. The younger one showed some promise, but after much discussion and prayer we didn't pursue it.

Our Board of Elders became involved in the development of a succession plan. At first, we decided to bring someone in who would take on some leadership responsibilities and then, during a period of a few years, grow into the position of Senior Pastor. Later, when a search committee was formed, it felt it would be hard to find the best candidate if he would not be able to come in and become the Senior Pastor when he arrived.

I did a lot of reading on transitioning leadership and talked about it with friends. Almost everyone questioned if it was wise for me to stay on staff after a new man was installed as my successor since I had been the founding and Senior Pastor for 25 years. Most authorities who had written on this subject agreed. I often heard during those days, "It's a no-brainer! You've got to leave when a new man takes over." The search committee even had me do a phone conversation with a consultant who concurred with this sentiment.

My feeling was that this proposition was based on three assumptions. First, the long-time Senior Pastor was not spiritually mature enough to turn the reins of leadership over to a younger man. Or he had some other insecurity that would make it difficult for him to walk through such a transition. Second, the candidate who would come in was not spiritually mature enough to take over the leadership without being intimidated by the former Senior Pastor. Third, the church was not mature enough to follow a new leader. I was not aware of any reference in the Bible that encouraged such a move. Nor did I feel it was wise to make an important decision based only on negatives.

It's true, we live in an imperfect world, and each of us is flawed. I had read and heard of many tragic cases where it did not work out well when a long-time Senior Pastor stayed on. I knew there would be many potential pitfalls if I stayed. However, I also felt that there would be some significant positive dynamics if the new man and I could work together in a complementary way.

My wife Mur and I were at a conference in Puerto Rico at the time the Board of Elders was going to finalize its decision. While there I woke up one night and thought of something that was not entirely new to me. It was the convergence of three important milestones that captured my attention. In less than a year we would be celebrating the twenty-fifth anniversary of the church and of my ministry as their founding Senior Pastor. Then, two weeks later, I would be celebrating my sixty-fifth birthday.

The plan that crystallized in my mind seemed simple and workable. I would serve as Senior Pastor until the twenty-fifth anniversary was celebrated and then continue until my successor was installed. At that time I would remain on staff as Minister át Large.

I probably should have written a note to remember but I didn't think I would forget what was so clear in my mind. I promptly went back to sleep. In the morning I shared with Mur the plan that had come together so clearly in my mind during the middle of the night. The moment I finished sharing it with her she said, "I like that!" We prayed about it and discussed it some more in order to be sure we both understood clearly what I should suggest to the board in an email. Once settled, I went down to the business center at the hotel, got on the Internet, and sent the board chairman the email.

This light in the night for living in the day brought both of us great peace and joy. In fact, we decided to go out and celebrate. We were staying close to some very nice hotels on the shore of the beautiful waters of the Caribbean. We selected one hotel and searched for its restaurant that overlooked the beach. We splurged with a special lunch as we celebrated our decision. When we got back home it was no surprise to us that the board was in agreement with this plan.

A little more than a year later, four months after the twenty-fifth anniversary celebration, the new Senior Pastor, Jamie Rasmussen, was installed, and I was commissioned as the Minister at Large. Throughout that year and since, Mur and I have enjoyed a very real peace that has helped us walk through this transition with greater ease than we ever expected. It also has been a testimony of God's grace in our church and community.

Our new Senior Pastor is a young man who grew up in our area. I had the joy of baptizing both Jamie and his wife Kim more than 20 years ago and later marrying them. He had served as an intern with us for one summer while pursuing his education. We maintained contact with each other throughout the ensuing years and now we were able to complement each other's ministries within the same congregation.

I've reflected on this experience and realized 'that the light in the night while in Puerto Rico was not something that happened in a vacuum. There were years of thought, prayer, discussion, reading, decision making, and adjusting to those decisions. Yet, during that whole process, lasting a few years, I had never connected the three dots of a double anniversary and my sixty-fifth birthday, nor had anyone else. The epiphany of seeing them aligned brought resolution. And the consensus of that resolution for the Board of Elders and my wife and me has helped us and the congregation go forth to continue building God's kingdom.

I believe many of us go through a similar process but are not looking for God to break through in His time to help us see what He is about to do. Proverbs 16:9 says,

"In his heart a man plans his course, but the Lord determines his steps."

God often uses His Word to help us understand what He is ordering for us. That's why Psalm 1:1-3 declares that we should meditate on God's law (Word) day and night if we want our lives to be fulfilling and fruitful. The Word of God might come alive to you and give you insight and direction in your situation during the day, but often He enlightens you during the night. We should prepare ourselves for that and be ready to reflect on what we sense He is saying to us. We then need to commit ourselves to living it out in faith and obedience.

You might think that Jesus, God the Son, would not need light in the night, for living in the day, but you'd be wrong. In Luke 6:12 it says,

"One of those days Jesus went out to a mountainside to pray and spent the night praying to God."

It doesn't say that He received any specific light for living the next day in harmony with His Father's will. But it is interesting to note that the next day was rather significant. Listen to what happened:

"When morning came, he called his disciples to him and chose twelve of them whom he also designated apostles."
(Luke 6:13)

The men who would lay the foundation of the church were chosen after Jesus spent the previous night in prayer. I don't believe this was a mere coincidence. I believe Jesus had spent much time thinking and praying about this. He knew each of these men. He had watched them respond to His call and teaching. It was after all that preparation that He received light in the night, for living, choosing the disciples, the next day.

How did I come to this conclusion? These were the men God the Father had chosen and given to Jesus according to His prayer as recorded in John 17:6:

> *"I have revealed you to those whom you gave me out of the world. They were yours; you gave them to me and they have obeyed your word."*

He also shared His heart with His heavenly Father in the garden of Gethsemane the night in which He was betrayed. Listen to the struggle He endured:

> *"They went to a place called Gethsemane, and Jesus said to his disciples, 'Sit here while I pray.' He took Peter, James and John along with him, and he began to be deeply distressed and troubled. 'My soul is overwhelmed with sorrow to the point of death,' he said to them. 'Stay here and keep watch.' Going a little farther, he fell to the ground and prayed that if possible the hour might pass from him. 'Abba, Father,' he said, 'everything is possible for you. Take this cup from me. Yet not what I will, but what you will.' Then he returned to his disciples and found them sleeping. 'Simon,' he said to Peter, 'are you asleep? Could you not keep watch for one hour? Watch and pray so that you will not fall into temptation. The spirit is willing, but the body is weak.' Once more he went away and prayed the same thing. When he came back, he again found them sleeping, because their eyes were heavy. They did not know what to say to him. Returning the third time,*

he said to them, 'Are you still sleeping and resting? Enough! The hour has come. Look, the Son of Man is betrayed into the hands of sinners. Rise! Let us go! Here comes my betrayer.'" (Mark 14:32-42)

During this agonizing ordeal in the garden Jesus received light in the night while praying to His Father. This enabled Him to go forward to fulfill His mission the next day, to die for our sins on the cross.

The disciples on the other hand slept during those agonizing moments. Jesus had invited them to share His burden. But fatigue overtook them. Even when awakened and warned about the danger they were about to face, they dozed off again. This was a time to watch and pray. This was a time to receive light for action during that dark dangerous night. Not stirring themselves to stay awake, they missed the light and, consequently, blundered their way through the ensuing hours, deserting Jesus in His time of need. And in Peter's case, he denied his Lord three times.

The light Jesus gained during those moments in the garden, the disciples lost. There is a price to pay either way. When God awakens you in the night, pay the price of giving attention to what He wants to say to you, or you'll pay the price of failure by being unable to stay faithful in the face of danger or to be ready to buy up the opportunity before you.

It is hard to understand how the children of Israel did not trust in the Lord their God when He made His presence known in such a dramatic way. Once the tabernacle was set up, He made His presence obvious by having the cloud cover it.

"From evening till morning the cloud above the tabernacle looked like fire...Whenever the cloud lifted from above the Tent, the Israelites set out; wherever the

cloud settled, the Israelites encamped. At the Lord's command the Israelites set out, and at his command they encamped. As long as the cloud stayed over the tabernacle, they remained in camp...Whether by day or by night, whenever the cloud lifted, they set out..." (Numbers 9:15-23)

How simple and straightforward. It would seem that determining God's will was a no-brainer. But it does take a certain amount of trust to set out or encamp at His command. You might want to consider comfort issues from your own perspective. Or you might think that moving out or encamping could be dangerous. Or maybe God will lift the cloud just as you have fallen asleep after a hard day's work. Or consider a woman giving birth to a child and hours later having to move on. The obvious isn't always the easiest. Attitudes don't always fall in line with clear, simple, straightforward directions.

Some of the places where the cloud settled were hot and dry with no apparent source of water. How could two to three million people survive there? And manna, though miraculously provided each morning, for some got unattractive after awhile. We shouldn't be too critical, however, in our opinion of these people.

I've done a lot of traveling throughout the years. There have been some exciting experiences. But a good bit of the time traveling is quite boring and tiring. The expectations of people you visit are not always what you had in mind. Just when you're ready to rest, they might have something planned. They're confident or assume you'd surely want to experience what they have planned. Or maybe you had something planned and you can't understand why they're not as excited about it as you are. That's life. It's unpredictable. Similarly, determining God's will is not always as easy or obvious as we might expect.

Take Paul's experience described in Acts 16. He and Silas had retraced the places Paul and Barnabas had visited on their first outreach trip. They recruited a young man, Timothy, to join them. After seeing the believers in each church and encouraging them, they set out to reach new territory. They *"traveled throughout the region of Phrygia and Galatia, having been kept by the Holy Spirit from preaching the word in the province of Asia. When they came to the border of Mysia, they tried to enter Bithynia, but the Spirit of Jesus would not allow them to. So they passed by Mysia and went down to Troas."* (Act s16:6-8)

They were not allowed to preach in Asia. Apparently, they did preach in Phrygia and Galatia. But when they tried pushing into Bithynia to the north and then Mysia to the west, the Spirit would not allow them to. It's not clear how the Holy Spirit made it clear to Paul and Silas that they were not to preach in these various regions of what is now known as Turkey. There is no mention of opposition, such as they faced in some of the places they visited on the first outreach trip. Whatever the Holy Spirit did to hinder them, it was obviously clear enough to them so that they simply moved on.

By the time they got to Troas, I imagine they were somewhat confused. Had Jesus not commanded the disciples to go to the *whole* world and preach the gospel to all people? Paul was committed to going where the gospel had not been preached in order to give people an opportunity to experience new life in Christ (Romans 15:20).

I can see Paul going out to the beach at Troas to be alone with God and praying for guidance. As he prayed and waited for an answer in the cool quietness of the night, he *"...had a vision of a man of Macedonia standing and begging him, 'Come over to Macedonia and help us.' After Paul had seen the vision, we got ready at once to leave for Macedonia, concluding that God had called us to preach the gospel to them."* (Acts 16:9-10)

Paul clearly received light in the night for living in the day. And he didn't waste any time to live out the light he had received.

This was a turning point in the spread of the gospel. When they set out by sea and landed at Samothrace and then Neapolis, they were on the eastern boundary of Europe. Philippi was a Roman colony and the leading city of that district of Macedonia. This opened the door to Europe and, ultimately, to the whole world. The delays and prohibitions in Turkey were a part of God's plan to open up the western world to the spread of the gospel.

When Paul later visited Ephesus and taught there for two years, the area of Asia that the Holy Spirit had hindered them from reaching before was then reached by those whom Paul trained in the school of Tyrannus. God always knows what He is doing.

> *"In his heart a man plans his course, but the Lord determines his steps."* (Proverbs 16:9)

I have often been perplexed by the process of determining God's will for my life. Only with hindsight do we see more clearly how the Lord has determined our steps.

While a student at Moody Bible Institute, I met with George Verwer on Tuesday nights to pray for the country of Spain. While still a student, George founded an organization now known as Operation Mobilization. Shortly after graduation he went to Spain and opened a bookstore in Barcelona. He has continued a ministry there throughout the years.

Just a couple of years ago my daily radio program, translated and produced in Spanish, began being aired over a network of stations throughout Spain. We prayed together more than 40 years ago. God used George as a part of the answer to our prayers within months after graduating. He is using my radio program now as a part of the answer to those nighttime prayers almost half a century later. God knows what He's about. We pray and plan. He orders our steps.

When you are seeking God for guidance because you don't know where to go or what to do keep the following in mind:
1. Heart preparation to receive guidance is a process.
2. When developing a plan always leave room for God's input.
3. Expect God to give you light in His time. He often does this at night.
4. When He gives light be receptive and obedient.

Application Questions:
1. Have you ever had a nighttime experience when you were given insight to connect the dots in a decision you were wrestling with?
2. How did that light in the night affect that decision?
3. Describe how you lived out that decision in the days that followed.
4. Have you ever left undone something that God clearly showed you?
5. Are you presently facing a decision for which you want God's guiding light?

Suggested Prayer:
"Dear Father, I thank You that You know me and my circumstances thoroughly. In Psalm 139:16 it says that 'all the days ordained for me were written in your book before one of them came to be.' Help me to see and sense Your guiding light for the decision I am now facing, so that I might please You by doing Your will. In Jesus name, Amen."

Lud Golz

Chapter Two

Laying the Foundation:
Am I building on the Rock?

"He took him outside and said, 'Look up at the heavens and count the stars – if indeed you can count them.' Then he said to him, 'So shall your offspring be.' Abraham believed the Lord, and he credited it to him as righteousness." (Genesis 15:4-6)

It was during a tour my wife and I led to the Holy Land that I had a unique experience while in Bethlehem.

In preparing for the trip I contacted the president of Bethlehem Bible College, Dr. Bishara Awad, and told him that I would like to visit the school while there. When we got to Bethlehem I left the tour group and went to the college. Dr. Awad was busy when I arrived so he introduced me to a young professor, Yohanna Katanacho, who showed me around.

As Yohanna explained the ministry of the school, I asked him questions about himself and how it was he wound up teaching there. The more I talked to him the more impressed I was with him. His dark eyes flashed with enthusiasm as he shared how God had transformed his life. I immediately sensed he was a special servant of God.

What a change this was from his university days when he was an arrogant Palestinian and something of a radical. Growing up in a religious home he learned many good things. But he confessed that he was influenced by friends and by his own desire to have a life uncontrolled by religion. He became an active atheist, and on campus he targeted Christian students, taunting them for what he considered to be a ridiculous faith.

One night he had an unusual experience. He recalls, "At 3:00 a.m. I woke up hearing the bells of the churches of Jerusalem ringing. When I opened my eyes I felt a strange air penetrating my body! Then I discovered I was not able to move. My hands, neck and feet were paralyzed. I was not able to shout. I thought that I was dead. Trying to understand what was going on, I failed to find a logical explanation."

After lying there in despair for two hours he cried out to God, "If you restore me from this paralysis, I will make an effort to know you." God answered his prayer and restored his body functions. From then on he was afraid to say that God didn't exist.

He didn't make much progress in his search, however. The Bible confused him. Fear continued to grip him. During that time he was invited to some special meetings at a church in Jerusalem. The message he heard touched his heart but didn't resolve his intellectual questions. So, he responded by asking Christ to take care of his sins, and he promised to follow Him. But God would have to convince his mind.

It was during this time that he had another experience at night in which he had three vivid dreams. In the first dream he felt himself surrounded by scary, ferocious looking individuals who were threatening him. But there was someone in front of him in a white robe. He reached out and took hold of the hem of his robe. As long as he grabbed the hem of his robe and held on tightly, he felt safe.

The second dream was similar, only this time he found himself inside a protective, transparent box. As long as he remained in this box, he was safe even though surrounded by the scary, ferocious-looking individuals.

The third dream was in the same scary setting, but this time he found himself in the arms of the one in the white robe he had followed in the first dream. That person was strong and his face was compassionate and comforting. As long as he rested in his arms, he felt safe.

When he awoke from these dreams, he had the strong impression that this one who had held him in his arms was Jesus Christ. He told me that day, "The first thought that struck me was that this is the difference between deeds and grace. If you want to follow Jesus Christ with your efforts, you will lose Him. You can't keep holding on to His garment in your own strength. If you are in Christ (in the box), then He will carry you. This is grace. These dreams were the turning point in my life. I felt that God was personal. He won my heart and mind. I accepted Jesus Christ as my Savior and Lord. He died on the cross in my place. I was convinced by His grace."

Having affirmed his trust in Jesus Christ he began studying the Bible in earnest. He even started teaching other students in small groups at his university. After graduating he went to Wheaton Graduate School and then earned his master's degree from Trinity Seminary, Deerfield, Illinois. He returned to his Palestinian Arab people and began teaching at Bethlehem Bible College. He also continued to do outreach missions at the university in Bethlehem. A number of years later he married and then returned to Trinity Seminary to work on getting a Ph.D. so he would be better prepared to serve his Lord.

God transformed his life by giving him light in the night for living in the day.

Yohanna's experience is not as unusual as it might seem. Throughout the centuries many have had encounters with God, often during the night. There doesn't appear to be a clear pattern of preparation to anticipate the encounters. But whenever it has happened there was always a responsiveness, a readiness to interact and then process what impressed them. One of the first of such encounters in recorded history was when God called Abram to become the father of a nation favored and blessed by God. This plan is recorded in Genesis 12:2-3:

> *"I will make you into a great nation and I will bless you;*
> *I will make your name great, and you will be a blessing. I*
> *will bless those who bless you, and whoever curses you I*
> *will curse; and all peoples on earth will be blessed*
> *through you."*

Over time Abram began to wonder when God was going to do what He had promised. God spoke to him again in a vision:

> *"Do not be afraid, Abram, I am your shield,' your very*
> *great reward."* (Genesis 15:1)

Abram expressed his doubt about any reward coming to him as long as he remained childless. In fact, he remonstrated God by saying,

> *"'The one who will inherit my estate is Eliezer of*
> *Damascus? You have given me no children; so a servant*
> *in my household will be my heir.' Then the word of the*
> *Lord came to him: 'This man will not be your heir, but a*
> *son coming from your own body will be your heir.' He*
> *took him outside and said, 'Look up at the heavens and*

count the stars – if, indeed, you can count them.' Then he said to him, 'So shall your offspring be.' **Abram believed the Lord, and he credited it to him as righteousness.***"*
(Genesis 15:2-6, bold added)

This obviously was a nighttime experience. They went outside and looked up at the star-studded night sky. What he saw clarified and reconfirmed God's promise, and Abram believed. That became the night Abram was converted, or was declared righteous by God. This experience in Abram's life was not only the foundation for all God had promised to do for and through him. It was also foundational for all who would follow him in believing that God keeps His promises.

When God again confirmed His covenant in Genesis 17, He conferred on him a new name. Abram means exalted father. His new name, Abraham, means the father of many. Abraham believed God and he became the father of all who believe God.

What is the essence of this faith? It is the opposite of what we accomplish by relying on our own efforts. It is not performance by us, which leads to merit or reward. It is dependence on what someone else promises and provides. The essence of faith is in looking at what is impossible and being persuaded that God has the power to do what He promised, in spite of our being convinced that humanly it is not possible.

Abraham is the great example of this. Romans 4:19-21 reads,

"He faced the fact that his body was as good as dead – since he was about a hundred years old – and that Sarah's womb was also dead. Yet he did not waver through unbelief regarding the promise of God, but was strengthened in his faith and gave glory to God,

being fully persuaded that God had power to do what he had promised. "

Faith understands that God's provision of salvation is a gift to be accepted.Accepting what God promises to give us is the action of faith – what it does. Before going any further let me clarify something up front. When I say, what it does, I am not suggesting that you start working at living the faith life. Romans 4:5 says,

"To the man who does not work but trusts God who justifies the wicked. "

The radical idea is that the one who does not work but trusts God, experiences God's grace. This to many is scandalous. It's a stumbling block. But it is the truth nevertheless.

Paul introduces another contrast in Romans 4:18, which reads,

"Against all hope, Abraham in hope believed. "

Dr. Kenneth Wuest writes in his commentary on Romans, "Abraham's situation was beyond hope...Yet he based his expectation upon hope. His situation was beyond human hopes, but in spite of that he rested it upon hope in God." Notice that he turned from the bankruptcy of human potential and effort and turned instead to the total sufficiency of God. With God nothing is impossible. Or as Paul put it in Romans 4:17, he believed in *"the God who gives life to the dead and calls things that are not as though they were. "*

There is no basis for hope if we rely in any way upon human nature or effort. Our hope must be placed in God and His power to do what He has promised. Once that focus is in place, we are ready to look at what is said in Romans 5:17. The action of faith is a matter of receiving *"God's abundant provision of grace and of the gift of righteousness."*

The provision of salvation to meet us in our need as sinners is a gift. It will remain a gift only if we receive it by faith. If we try to earn it or pay for it after we receive it, then it is no longer a gift. It would then be merited. And that is diametrically the opposite of grace.

It is important to notice what Paul says in Romans 6:17:

> *"You wholeheartedly obeyed the form of teaching to which you were entrusted."*

When by faith you *"receive God's abundant provision of grace and of the gift of righteousness,"* your heart will be attuned to and want to obey the teaching to which you were entrusted. The action of faith opens the door for God to do a new thing in your innermost being, a spiritual rebirth, in which the Holy Spirit comes to dwell within you. He inclines your heart to the truth, enlightens your understanding of the truth, and then prompts you to obey the truth. The momentum created by the act of faith expresses itself in wholehearted obedience to the truth.

When we receive this gift of eternal life the Holy Spirit makes us new on the inside and prompts us to obey the truth wholeheartedly. Having said that does not mean that we are not tempted to revert to relying on human effort. It is a common failure. So, we need to be encouraged according to Romans 6:11 to count ourselves dead to sin but alive to God in Christ Jesus. The word translated "count" has the idea of reckoning, computing or taking into account. Faith is not a leap into the dark unknown. Faith grows out of a process in which we take into account what is true.

Believing what Paul said in Romans chapters 1-3 would be accepting the truth that, left to myself, I am hopelessly lost. And if I accept that truth, I will gladly listen to what God has promised to provide for my salvation from sin and its consequences. Taking into account that God has provided righteousness as a gift, I would be foolish not to receive it. And having received it, Paul says that I should consciously count on what this means to me personally. In other words the action of faith is to count on my belonging to God. I am His and He is mine. I can count on it.

According to Romans 4:3, *"Abraham believed God."* The God he believed in was *"the God who gives life to the dead and calls things that are not as though they were"* (verse 17). It is also the God *"who raised Jesus our Lord from the dead."* (verse 24)

Abraham believed in the Almighty, self-sufficient, miracle-working God of creation. This God had promised him a son through whom there would emerge a nation.

And even though he saw no human way that this could be possible, he believed that God had the power to do what He had promised.

With God, nothing is impossible. Placing faith in Him opens your heart so that God can do His promised work of grace in you. You also read in Romans 3:22 and 26 that we are to place our faith in Jesus Christ. Two specifics related to Jesus Christ are to be believed. In Romans 3:25 it mentions having faith in His blood, referring to His sacrifice of atonement on the cross. Later, in Romans 4:24 it refers to His being raised from the dead. It is clear that we are to have faith in the person, death and resurrection of Jesus Christ. Discount any one of these three pillars of the Christian faith and you do not have Christianity. If He is not who He claimed to be, or if He did not die and rise from the dead, our faith is in vain. We are still lost in our sins.

Paul put it this way in what some scholars believe incorporates the first Christian creed, dating back to only a few years after Christ's resurrection, recorded in 1 Corinthians 15:3-5:

> *"For what I received I passed on to you as of first importance: that Christ died for our sins according to the Scriptures, that he was buried, that he was raised on the third day according to the Scriptures, and that he appeared to Peter, and then to the Twelve. After that, he appeared to more than five hundred of the brothers at the same time, most of whom are still living, though some have fallen asleep. Then he appeared to James, then to all the apostles, and last of all he appeared to me also."*

Many have questioned the trustworthiness of this Gospel message and provision. But those who have trusted in and received this gift from God have not been disappointed.

Blaise Pascal, a brilliant 17th century mathematician, considered to be the father of the modern computer, took that step of faith. His experience was so dramatic that he did something unusual to memorialize it. He described his experience in a note that he wrote on a piece of paper and sewed it into the lining of his jacket: "Monday, 23 November, 1654. From about half past ten in the evening until about half past midnight – Fire. The God of Abraham, the God of Isaac, the God of Jacob. Not of the philosophers and intellectuals. Certitude, certitude. Jesus Christ... may I never be separated from Him."

Notice that this was a nighttime experience. He discovered light in the night for living in the day. Or better yet, he discovered the Light of the World, Jesus Christ, Who transformed his life for time and eternity. As a result, he shared that light with as many as he could, especially the intellectuals of his day.

Even today his jacket with his testimony sewn into the lining is kept in the archives of the Church of Saint-Germain-des-Pres. And his book, *Pensees*, continues to be read by inquiring minds all over the world.

You don't have to have a nighttime experience to establish a relationship with God. His grace is available at all times. The important thing is to remember the following:

1. God provides the foundation rock for your life, Jesus Christ.
2. You must accept that gift by faith and receive eternal life.
3. Build your life on this foundation by turning from the bankruptcy of human potential and effort and turning instead to the total sufficiency of God's provision.
4. Recognize that that provision includes the Holy Spirit who indwells all believers.
5. Trust the Holy Spirit to transform you into the person He wants you to be.

Application Questions:
1. Have you taken the step of faith where in prayer you asked Jesus Christ to become your Savior and Lord?
2. When did that happen, and how would you describe what happened in your own words?
3. Do you have assurance that the foundation has been laid for your life with God?
4. If you have not taken that step of faith, are you willing to take it now?
5. If you have, are you trusting the Holy Spirit to transform and build your life into the person He wants you to be?

Suggested Prayer:

"Dear heavenly Father, I thank You for Your love for me. I know that I have come short of Your standard of holiness and that I need forgiveness. Thank You for sending Your Son, Jesus Christ, to become my Savior by dying for my sins. I believe You raised Him from the dead to be a living Savior. I invite Him to come into my life, forgive my sins and take over the control of my life. I surrender to Him. Make me the person You want me to be. In Jesus name, Amen."

Lud Golz

Chapter Three

Unsettling:
Why Is This Happening
to Me?

"Even at night his mind does not rest." (Ecclesiastes 2:23)

I still remember going to bed many nights as a teenager feeling a lot like Job, who said, *"The night drags on, and I toss till dawn."* (Job 7:4)

Or more accurately, like David, who said, *"Day and night your hand is heavy upon me."* (Psalm 32:4)

You see, I grew up in a home where I was taught right from wrong. I was affirmed when I did right and disciplined when I did wrong. Early in life I realized that I did wrong more than I wanted to and right less than I should have.

I was taught that there was one, Jesus Christ, who would forgive me when I did wrong and would enable me to do right. But I needed to ask Him to come into my life by faith.

In my family's church we had special meetings every January when the focus was on calling people to take that step of faith. The year I was seven, no one responded to the invitation during these two weeks of meetings. Before the last night the Sunday school teachers gathered all their students and told them to respond when the invitation was given. I went forward with the rest of the kids, but nothing happened in my life.

The next year I went forward on my own accord, but like the previous year it was because I felt it was expected of us. Again, nothing really happened in my life. But when I was nine years old, I understood better. And when I went forward, I had the sense that God heard my prayer and gave me new spiritual life. It's not that I understood all that was involved at that point. And, unfortunately, I was not helped to understand it better in ways that I could readily respond to. Consequently, I didn't grow in my spiritual journey. During the years I was an early teen I got in with the wrong group of kids in my school and began doing things I knew were wrong. I didn't want to do them, yet I was attracted to them and got sucked into a downward spiral that brought deep conviction into my life.

That's when I remember going to bed and quietly sobbing myself to sleep, promising God that I would be better tomorrow. But when tomorrow came I went down the same path. The longer this happened the more difficult it became to believe that God would forgive me. It was devastatingly unsettling.

When the annual evangelistic meetings took place at my church during my senior year in high school, I wanted to get things right with God. But each night when the invitation was given, I felt glued to my seat. My parents invited the evangelist over for dinner before the last night of the services. I convinced myself that I would talk to him that night. But the night before, as I sat in the service, my mind wandered, thinking about unrelated things. All of a sudden I found myself whispering a prayer – "Help me concentrate on what this guy is saying." Opening that crack in the door of my heart was all God needed. I didn't hear much of what the evangelist was saying. I already knew what I needed to do and when the invitation was given I took the step David describes in verse 5 of Psalm 32:

> *"Then I acknowledged my sin to you and did not cover up my iniquity. I said, 'I will confess my transgressions to the Lord' – and you forgave the guilt of my sin."*

That decision set the stage for what God wanted to do with my life. There had been a log jam in my life, and the pressure was tightening the jam. When I recognized and acknowledged this God masterfully released the critical log, the jam loosened and the flow of God's purpose for my life began again. I received light in the night for living in the day.

As I read through the Bible I found that some, like Job, had unsettling experiences that weren't caused by sin and guilt. Job was identified by God as *"blameless and upright; he feared God and shunned evil."* (Job 1:2)

He was a wealthy man who was faithful to his family and to God. Suddenly, the bottom dropped out in his life. He lost everything except his wife. His strong faith was shaken as he desperately tried to make some sense out of it all. As he debated his fate with his friends, he was heard to say, *"The night drags on, and I toss till dawn."* (Job 7:4) The nighttime despair drove him to wish daylight would not arrive. He wasn't sure he could face another day. But it came and went, day and night after day and night. It all seemed like one long, dark, despairing, stormy night.

Then, out of the storm raging in his mind and heart, God started asking him some rhetorical questions (Job 38 through 41). Job had argued and tried to answer the accusations of his friends. But when God spoke, he was quiet. It was an unsettling, stupefying silence before God. In somber humility he finally replied to the Lord:

"I know that you can do all things; no plan of yours can be thwarted. You asked, 'Who is this that obscures my counsel without knowledge?' Surely I spoke of things I did not understand, things too wonderful for me to know. You said, 'Listen now, and I will speak; I will question you, and you shall answer me.' My ears had heard of you but now my eyes have seen you. Therefore I despise myself and repent in dust and ashes." (Job 42:2-6)

Job's unsettling nightmare set the stage for him to receive light in the night for living in the day. When he acknowledged his unworthiness and declared his faith in God's sovereignty and grace his life was transformed and abundantly blessed, more than what he had ever known before. Once his nightmare was over and he was walking in the light God had shown him, he was able to bless others in a new way, even those who had unjustly accused him (Job 42:7-17). When they confessed their wrongdoing Job prayed for them, and the Lord answered his prayer and was merciful to them.

Joni Eareckson Tada was an active teenager when she had a swimming accident. She dived off a raft and unexpectedly hit bottom with her head, leaving her paralyzed. After being rescued and rushed to the hospital she was examined and given the devastating news that she would be a quadriplegic the rest of her life. Initially, she didn't want to live. She was angry with God and felt hopelessly abandoned.

Later, Joni realized she was not alone. Her family stood with her, and so did her friends. One particular night a close friend, Cindy, was visiting, trying to comfort her. Not knowing what to say she finally blurted out that Jesus knows what she was feeling. She pointed out that Joni wasn't the only one who was paralyzed. Jesus experienced it too.

Almost impulsively Joni exploded, wondering what she was talking about.

Cindy explained that being nailed on the cross Christ was immobilized. But he could feel the pain of raw flesh against the rugged cross. Any moving, ever so slight, would only aggravate the pain. But the impulse to change positions was futile. The nails paralyzed him.

New light gradually dawned in Joni's mind. Yes, Jesus had experienced similar sensations as she was experiencing. He really did understand. And that comforted her. The love of her family and friends was precious. But now she sensed God's presence and love in a new way. Slowly, she began to see her seemingly hopeless condition as a luxury. Before she viewed God as intruding into her agenda of dating, career plans and other activities she enjoyed. Now her agenda was stripped away. Alone, paralyzed, hopeless, she was left with God. He was her only hope and gradually she realized He was all she needed.

That night she thought, "I have no other identity but God, and He's enough. What an overwhelming phenomenon – a personal God, who created the universe, is living in my life. If my life will ever be attractive and worthwhile, He'll have to do it – I can't do it without Him." This light in the night for living in the day energized her.

Gradually, Joni's perspective on life changed even though her condition remained the same. God had a purpose for her life and enabled her to fulfill it as she trusted and obeyed. In the years that followed, those gifts have multiplied, and as she has used them God has touched countless others who are physically, emotionally and mentally challenged. She has encouraged many with her inspiring testimony through the many facets of her organization, "Joni and Friends," and through her writing, speaking and painting.

God has used her unsettling experience to transform her life, then many others through her.

Horatio G. Spafford was a real estate magnet who lost his fortune the night of the great Chicago fire of 1871. He also lost his son at that time to scarlet fever. Almost overcome with grief he buried himself in the task of rebuilding the city and helping the thousands who were homeless.

Two years later he felt he and his family needed a break. He decided to go to Europe to enjoy a vacation. But just as they were ready to leave he was detained by an urgent business matter in New York, so he sent his wife and four daughters on, promising to join them as soon as possible. During the night, as their boat, the luxurious French liner *Ville du Havre,* smoothly plied the sea, they suddenly collided with an iron sailing vessel. Jolted from their bunks the passengers realized that their ship was tilting and water was pouring in through gaping holes. Panic struck as they clamored for safety, not knowing where to find it in the darkness. Things happened too fast for most of the passengers to be rescued. Within two hours two hundred twenty-six passengers went down with the mighty ship, including Spafford's four daughters. His wife Anna was found, hardly conscious but hanging on to a piece of the wreckage. She was one of only forty seven survivors. When they landed in Cardiff, Wales, she cabled her husband, "Saved Alone."

He left to join his wife as quickly as possible. One cold wintry night the captain went to Spafford and took him outside. "I believe we are now passing over the place," he said, "where the *Ville du Havre* went down." He stood there as silently as a sentinel. Finally, numb from all he had been through he went back to his cabin and tried to go to sleep. As he restlessly tossed in his bed he reflected further about his loss. Gradually a thought emerged. He concluded, "It is well; the will of God be done."

Later he wrote the well known hymn based on those words:

"When peace like a river, attendeth my way,
when sorrows like sea billows roll;
whatever my lot,
Thou hast taught me to say,
'It is well, it is well with my soul.'"

Through a series of very unsettling experiences he had received light in the night that enabled him to go on living in the day. The strength he found enriched the lives of many through this hymn.

We might face unsettling experiences that are caused by our sinning against God and resisting His conviction. At other times unsettling experiences come at us from out of nowhere, totally unexpected. If we have wandered from God we need to repent and return to Him. If God has allowed trials to come our way we need to trust God to get us through them and learn from them. They are often the means of our greatest growth.

Application Questions:
1. Have you ever had an unsettling experience, caused by your own bad choices? Has it been resolved? How?
2. Have you ever had an unsettling experience that came out of nowhere? Has it been resolved? How?
3. What are the lessons you have learned from these experiences?
4. In what way, if any, would you respond differently now if you faced similar circumstances?

Suggested Prayer if your unsettling experience has been cause by your own bad choices:

"Dear Father, I have felt the pressure of your loving, firm hand of conviction in my heart and mind. Forgive me for resisting your love. I confess my sin. Please forgive me and fill me with a sense of your acceptance. Make me the person you want me to be and enable me to live my life in a way that would please you. In Jesus name, Amen."

Suggested Prayer if your unsettling experience came on you unexpectedly:

"Dear Father, I don't understand why this has happened to me, but I trust in You to be with me and work through this experience to make me the person you want me to be. Give me the strength and patience to endure and to obey You, so that Your will and purpose will be accomplished. In Jesus name, Amen."

Chapter Four

Setting the Stage: Can Anything Good Come of This?

"Weeping may remain for a night, but rejoicing comes in the morning." (Psalm 30:5)

I will never forget Labor Day weekend, 1976. That year had been a prolonged, anguishing nightmare.

The previous fall I had come down with viral pneumonia. At first I felt I could shake off what I thought was just a bad cold. There was much to do. After almost four years at our church, we had seen significant progress in every measurable way. Attendance and budget had tripled. And now we were getting ready to dedicate our new facility that would triple the size of our building.

My brother, Pete, and his wife Gail were visiting us to help celebrate this milestone in our ministry. Friday morning I was feeling worse than anytime during the previous month. In fact, I was experiencing double vision when I got to my office. But I kept it to myself. When my associate, Ken, came in and saw me, he was concerned and asked what was wrong. Totally out of character I yelled at him, "Get out of here!"

Mur planned a nice lunch for us and invited Ken and his wife Dotty to join us. As lunch started, I felt nauseated, so I excused myself and started to go to my bedroom. After a few steps I keeled over and landed on our living room sofa. Everyone was alarmed. Mur and Pete got me up, took me out to the car and drove me as quickly as possible to the hospital. I was going downhill fast as I waited to be admitted. Once in my hospital bed I drifted in and out of consciousness.

The church had brought in a special musical group and a well-known speaker. While all these festivities were going on I was in the hospital oblivious to it all. Not knowing what might happen to me, Mur was traumatized. With company and four children to take care of, all worried about me, she went to the services, but felt numb through it all. The doctors also worried. They ran all kinds of tests, including a spinal tap, trying to find out what was wrong. Later they told us that I was very close to dying from viral pneumonia.

For two weeks I slowly recovered in the hospital. This was followed by another two weeks of resting at home. The doctor was so worried that I might try to leave my room and go to church that he came to our church the first Sunday to check things out. I saw him from the bedroom window of our parsonage. This was one of the few light moments during that time. I was humored to think that it would take this much to get him to come to church!

The second month I was only able to get to the office part time. I noticed that the old guard in the church had taken us back to the more rigid, traditional style that characterized the church before I had come there.

My wife was more discerning than I was, and she began to feel things getting worse at the church. There was a movement that to her was like an emerging dark cloud. I felt that with time I could address the issues and work with the leadership to get things back on track. I was wrong. She was right.

I vividly remember a board meeting right after coming back from vacation in which I was accused of lying to the board about a commitment I had made to teach at an evening Bible school on my day off. Their conclusion was based on a third party comment. Great pressure was put on me to confess wrongdoing. I tried to see things from their perspective. The problem for me was that I had not lied.

As I walked out of that meeting I felt battered, beaten and abandoned. When I finally came home, I told Mur I didn't know how I was going to lead the prayer meeting two nights later, let alone preach on the following Sunday. I was devastated.

The next morning I got a call from my brother Pete. He shared that my father's health was failing. After chatting awhile I hung up. Mur, who had been on the phone with me, asked me, "Do you think Pete was telling you, if you want to see your Dad before he dies you'd better come soon?"

"I didn't pick that up."

"I believe that's what he was trying to tell you," she insisted.

Stunned, I dialed him up and point blank asked him if that is what he was trying to say to me?

"Yes," he replied. "I don't think Dad's going to live much longer."

I immediately got on the phone and was able to get tickets to Vancouver, Canada. We left the next morning. I didn't have to figure out how to get through prayer meeting that night nor the following Sunday morning service. Even though it was a sad time visiting with family at my Dad's bedside, it did provide a reprieve from what I was facing at the church.

When I returned, a false rumor was spreading that I had said something to one of the leaders over the phone that just wasn't true. I know because I had my wife listening in on the conversation I had with him.

Within a week my father died. The following Sunday was our wedding anniversary, but we were not celebrating. Everything was so difficult I couldn't understand it. We were confused, but the Lord sustained us through it. That Sunday I finished preaching through an eight month series of messages on the Sermon on the Mount. What I didn't realize yet was that this day would be a final turning point for me and my wife at that church.

As I was getting ready to leave for home after the evening service, two leaders asked to talk with me in my office. As the conversation began they again falsely accused me, this time based on stories they got from my secretary. In the process of the accusations, they began to include my wife.

Mur had gone home with the kids after the service. As she prepared a snack for them she was prompted by the Lord to come up to my office. When she approached, she heard them accusing her of untrue stories. It was devastating to her. She didn't know what to do. Fortunately, she just returned home, but was determined that this was it. She couldn't take any more.

I, too, concluded, before I left the office that night, that we couldn't go on any longer. When I got home, it was clear that, though painful, both of us had received light in the night for living in the days before us.

For more than half a year we had prayed our way through the struggle that was going on. Preparing the messages on the Sermon on the Mount during those months provided guidance for walking through the maze of questions, emotions and disappointments. We even had long time friends visit us during this time. As they listened and observed what was going on, they suggested that sometimes God allows difficult times to dislodge us from what otherwise we would never consider leaving.

As we talked and prayed that night, we were not aware of where God was leading us, only that He wanted us to leave. He was closing a door, but we were still in the dark about what door He would open. We finally decided to tell Ken and Dotty the next morning that I was resigning, and then come home to tell our kids.

The next morning, after spending time with Ken and Dotty, we came home. Mur pulled things together and with the kids started packing. I got alone in my office and prepared my letter of resignation to present to the leadership of the church that evening.

We had no idea where we would be going or what I would be doing. The only plan we had was to start the process of moving on. That included me preparing what I determined to say my last Sunday as the pastor of the church.

Within days after resigning I had a couple of calls for interviews. I didn't have peace pursuing one of the opportunities. When I pursued the other, a position with a mission agency, the president invited me to meet him at his cabin on a Christian campground. The job they were offering fitted my experience and passion well, but I realized that it would require a move to another state, and then I would be traveling most of the time. That would be asking too much of my family after the trauma we had gone through.

Something we did not contemplate or anticipate began to happen almost immediately. The night we got home from visiting the mission executive we called a friend from our church. He told us a group of the folk from our church was meeting at a home and asked if I would come over. I was tired from the trip, but agreed to meet with them. I found out that they were talking about starting a new church in the area and they wanted me to consider becoming their pastor. I let them know immediately that I was not interested. Then they asked if I would be willing to meet with them and help them develop a plan for this church startup. Hesitantly, I agreed to meet with them.

While still in limbo, Mur and I decided to do some house searching. Our time for living in the parsonage was coming to an end and school was starting for our four children within weeks. When we found a home we liked, even though we had no assurance of a job, we signed a contract for the home on Saturday of Labor Day weekend.

The next day the new church start was having its first meeting, and I had agreed to be the speaker. After the service the leaders of the group again asked me if I would consider becoming their pastor. Since I needed work, especially after signing the contract for the house, I decided to accept their offer. I must admit, it was a rather pragmatic decision.

As I write this, we have served our church, Fellowship Bible Church of Chagrin Falls, Ohio, for 31 years. We celebrated my twenty-fifth anniversary as Senior Pastor a few year ago, and now continue serving there as Minister at Large. These years have been a wonderful, fruitful journey for us and for the church. To God be the Glory.

God took one of our darkest moments and, in the midst of our agony, provided light in the night for living in the days, weeks, and months that followed. Yes, we can agree with the Psalmist, though *"weeping may remain for a night...rejoicing comes in the morning."* (Psalm 30:5)

What we experienced is not as unusual as it might seem. Remember Jacob running away from his family for fear that his brother Esau might kill him? He had reason to run. He had outwitted his brother of his birthright. Then he lied to his aging, gullible father in order to steal his brother's blessing as the older son. He ran for his life because his brother wanted to get even with him by killing him.

Genesis 28:11-15 tells us what followed.

"When he reached a certain place, he stopped for the night because the sun had set. Taking one of the stones there, he put it under his head and lay down to sleep. He had a dream in which he saw a stairway resting on the earth, with its top reaching to heaven, and the angels of God were ascending and descending on it. There above it stood the Lord, and he said: 'I am the Lord, the God of your father Abraham and the God of Isaac. I will give you and your descendents the land on which you are lying. Your descendants will be like the dust of the earth, and you will spread out to the west and to the east, to the north and to the south. All peoples on earth will be blessed through you and your offspring. I am with you and will watch over you wherever you go, and I will bring you back to this land. I will not leave you until I have done what I have promised.'"

God, in a unique way, was reaffirming to Jacob the promise he gave to his grandfather Abraham many years before. Jacob's response to this light in the night was to set up as a pillar the stone he had rested his head on during the night and to pour oil on top of it. He called this place Bethel. He worshiped God there, and then made a vow. It was conditional, but it was an affirmation of commitment and faith.

When he finally arrived at his mother's family homestead, he was welcomed. When they gave him a job he decided to stay. While working for Laban, his mother's brother, he noticed how beautiful his daughter Rachel was. When he asked for her hand in marriage, Laban agreed to give her to him if he worked for him for seven years. When the seven years were over, Laban deceived him by giving him Leah, Rachel's older sister. Though deeply hurt, Jacob agreed to work for Laban another seven years to get Rachel as his wife. This stressful relationship with Laban led to Jacob spending many years in frustration and disgust. He finally decided to leave and return to where his brother Esau lived.

On his way back, as he got close to his brother's home, he was afraid of what he might encounter. He set up an elaborate welcoming parade of his family, servants and possessions, hoping this would assuage his brother Esau.

After he sent them on he withdrew by himself.

*"That night...Jacob was left alone, and a man wrestled with him till daybreak. When the man saw that he could not overpower him, he touched the socket of Jacob's hip so that his hip was wrenched as he wrestled with the man. Then the man said 'Let me go, for it is daybreak.' But Jacob replied, 'I will not let you go unless you bless me.' The man asked him, 'What is your name?' 'Jacob,' he answered. Then the man said, 'Your name will no longer be Jacob, but Israel, because **you have struggled with God** and with men and have overcome'...Then he blessed him there"* (Genesis 32:22-29, bold added).

When the brothers finally met they were reconciled. They even had the opportunity of working together in burying their father, Isaac, who died as a very old man.

Another example of God setting the stage for something new is Joseph who was sold into slavery by his brothers. Why? Because he shared with them a dream he had about God's plan for his life. In the dream he indicated he would overshadow everyone else in his family. In spite, his brothers sold him into slavery and he was taken to Egypt. While there he was bought by Potiphar, an

Egyptian who was one of Pharaoh's officials, the captain of the guard. Joseph faithfully served his master. On one occasion his master's wife tried to have an affair with him. When he refused and ran out of the house, she falsely accused him. His master, believing her story, was furious and had Joseph thrown into jail.

God gave Joseph the ability to interpret dreams. One night two fellow prisoners had dreams that Joseph interpreted for them. Then, sometime later, Pharaoh had a dream. The cupbearer, whose dream Joseph had interpreted accurately, remembered his experience and shared it with Pharaoh. Joseph was called in and asked to interpret Pharaoh's dream. Joseph replied, *"I cannot do it, but God will give Pharaoh the answer he desires."*

When Pharaoh shared his dream Joseph gave him the interpretation. Then he gave him counsel in the light of the interpretation. Pharaoh was so impressed with Joseph's counsel that he appointed him Prime Minister of his kingdom. The dreams Joseph had as a boy began to be fulfilled before his very eyes. In his exalted position he was able to have his family immigrate to Egypt and be taken care of during the time of famine Joseph had predicted. Truly God had given him light in the night many times so that he could live by faith with wisdom and authority.

There also is the story of Esther. Following her uncle Mordecai's advice she became King Xerxes' queen. Later Mordecai discovered that Haman, the king's right hand man, had persuaded the king to seal an edict that would extinguish the Jewish nation. He sent word to Esther challenging her that, though it would be risky, she should not remain silent about this edict. He was confident that God would find someone to stand in the gap if she didn't.

"Who knows," he said, "but that you have come to royal position for such a time as this." (Esther 4:14)

Though fearful, facing the possible extinction of the people of Israel, she relented and called for a three day fast, day and night. After that she would risk her life by appearing before the king uninvited. That action would be against the law, but she was ready to perish if necessary to plead for her people.

When she came before the king he welcomed her and asked what she wanted. Rather than blurt out her desire she invited him to a banquet along with Haman, the one who had masterminded the ruthless edict to kill all the Jews in the kingdom. At the banquet the king again asked her what she wanted. Confidently, she repeated her invitation for them to come to a banquet the following night.

> *"That night the king could not sleep; so he ordered the book of the chronicles, the record of his reign, to be brought in and read to him. It was found recorded there that Mordecai had exposed Bigthana and Teresh, two of the king's officers who guarded the doorway, who had conspired to assassinate King Xerxes. 'What honor and recognition has Mordecai received for this?' the King asked. 'Nothing has been done for him,' his attendants answered."* (Esther 6:1-3)

Haman came to the palace the next morning to ask the king for Mordecai's head. As he entered the court the king enquired about who was in the court?

> *"His attendants answered, 'Haman is standing in the court.' 'Bring him in,' the king ordered. When they ushered him in to the king, he asked him, 'What should be done for the man the king delights to honor?'"* (Esther 6:6)

Thinking it was he whom the king wanted to honor, Haman suggested a rather extravagant display with royal robe and horse and crest. He was to be led through the streets of the capital decked out like this with one proclaiming before him, *"This is what is done for the man the king delights to honor!"*

You can almost feel the dismay Haman felt when the king said,

> *"Go at once, get the robe and the horse and do just as you have suggested for Mordecai the Jew, who sits at the king's gate. Do not neglect anything you have recommended."* (Esther 6:10)

After this was done Mordecai returned to the king's gate, but Haman, humiliated and crushed, went home only to have his family and friends predict that he would come to ruin.

Later that night Haman had to go to the banquet. While at the banquet, Esther pleaded for her life and that of her people. When she exposed Haman's evil plans to the king he was enraged and left the banquet to think.

Haman, fearing for his life, pled with Esther to intervene.

When the king returned to the banquet hall he saw Haman at Esther's side on the couch where she was reclining. Unable to contain his anger he exclaimed, *"Will he even molest the queen while she is with me in the house?"*

That's all he had to say. Immediately the king's attendants covered Haman's face. He was as good as dead. Finding out about the gallows Haman had built to hang Mordecai, the king ordered him to be hung on it instead. Satisfied that justice had been done, his anger subsided. Esther was given Haman's estate and Mordecai was given authority to write an edict and seal it with the king's signet ring, giving the Jews in the kingdom the right to defend themselves against Haman's edict to extinguish them.

Yes, when God sets the stage to act, He might even choose to give light in the night to a pagan king in order to have him live it out in the day of God's appointment. And the same light would enlighten and embolden the people of God to protect themselves from the threat of the edict. This they did when the day came for the edict to be implemented.

Their deliverance was such a significant event in the minds of the Jews it has been commemorated down through the centuries by the Jewish people as the Feast of Purim. Truly, it was light in the night for living in the day.

God has a plan for each of us. He works at setting the stage for His plan to be implemented in our lives. Often this happens during stressful and even hurtful experiences. Sometimes He even uses problems we create by our own bad decisions to close some doors and open others so that we consider options we'd otherwise never be open to.

Application Questions:

1. Have you ever had a traumatic experience that God turned around to set the stage for a significant new opportunity?
2. What was the most helpful thing you did to prepare yourself for getting through it?
3. Was there anything you wish you had done differently?
4. What was the most helpful thing others did to enable you to get through it?
5. What lesson learned through the process was most helpful for tackling the new opportunity God was opening up for you?

Suggested Prayer:

"Dear loving Father, thank you for allowing me to experience this trial that you are using/have used to prepare me for the opportunity you are opening up before me. Help me to remember the lessons you are teaching me and to apply them to my life as I pursue new opportunities. Please order my steps so Your will is accomplished. In Christ's name, Amen."

Lud Golz

Chapter Five

Cry Out to God: Do I Have to Go Through This?

"Arise, cry out in the night as the watches of the night begin; pour out your heart like water in the presence of the Lord." (Lamentations 2:19)

My mother grew up in a rural German community about 30 miles north east of Warsaw, Poland, in the early 20th century. Since her family was very poor she was sent out early in life to be a servant in a wealthy home in Warsaw. She used to tell us kids many hair-raising adventures she had where God answered prayer in miraculous ways.

As a teenager she returned home and worked at home weaving flax all day. By evening her fingers were bleeding from the rough flax threads. After a long day at the weaving wheel she often would quietly go out at night behind the barn and cry out to God to comfort and sustain her.

While she was a teenager, a revival broke out in the region where she lived, and though she was told not to go to the services she went anyway. I remember talking with her just before she died, asking questions about her life experience. In more detail than I could ever remember before, she shared how she came to believe in Jesus Christ as her Savior. She went to a prayer meeting one night in a neighbor's home. All of a sudden she felt herself being forced by an unseen hand to kneel before God and pray. As she articulated her prayer, I recognized it as a Catechism doctrinal statement of faith. In a flash her life was changed.

When her mother found out about her going to the meetings, she warned her and her sisters not to go anymore and threatened them if they did. They went anyway and were beaten for it. They persisted in their commitment and were baptized in a river in the cold early spring. As they went home with wet clothes, they realized their mother would be furious with them.

My mother's younger sister hid in a nearby haystack. As their mother searched for her, she grabbed a large fork and began poking in the haystack. Instinctively my mother cried out to God in desperation and was emboldened to do what was unheard of in her day and culture. She turned and confronted her mother, grabbed the pitchfork out of her hands and demanded, "Never touch us again!"

Amazingly, her mother never threatened or touched them again. They went on to grow into strong followers of Christ. As a young woman my mother emigrated to Canada, married my father, who also had come from Poland, and started their family in Vancouver, Canada.

During those final conversations I had with my mother, she told me how she dedicated me to the Lord while I was still in her arms. As we grew, my brother and I gave her plenty of reason to pray. She was fervent and faithful in her prayer life, but we persisted in doing things boys do. As mentioned earlier I made a decision to trust in Jesus Christ when I was nine years old, but was not followed up in a way that was relevant to the youth culture in which I was raised. My parents had never gone to school and didn't understand some of the things we faced in school.

My brother and I were into sports. Our parents never played any sports, nor did they understand them. It was not that they hindered or limited our involvement, but we couldn't share our experiences with them. We didn't expect them to be a part of that dimension of our lives.

Through all of this I got in with the wrong crowd. I was on the edge of things they were into -- close enough to be affected. I was experiencing what Paul the Apostle said in 1 Corinthians 15:33, *"Bad company corrupts good character."*

I remember one incident that shattered my parents, especially my mother. Having dressed up in a new black suit, I went to a New Year's Eve party after a watch-night service at our church. While there I drank too much. I didn't remember most of what happened that night. I vomited all over my clothes. When I was dropped off at home, I punched out a window in the back basement door to get in. Groggily, I climbed up the stairs to my room and with my clothes on flopped into bed, oblivious of what had happened.

I found out the next morning that my parents had taken off my clothes. Then my mother washed them in her tears. Heartsick, she cried out to God, "If this is what I get after praying all these years, I quit."

For days she couldn't say anything to me, but I knew she was devastated, and I felt totally responsible. Later she confided that when she resolved to quit praying for me that night, she got the strong impression from God, "My dear child, your responsibility is to pray. My responsibility is to answer prayer. Don't worry about My responsibility. Just be faithful in *your* responsibility to pray."

This light in the night, provided my mother with encouragement to keep on praying and living by faith during the dark days ahead. Less than a half month later I returned to Jesus

Christ and renewed my commitment to Him. He began to do what Paul described in Ephesians 2:10:

> *"For we are God's workmanship, created in Christ Jesus to do good works, which God prepared in advance for us to do."*

Fortunately for me, that New Year's Eve was the only time in my life that I got "bombed." God protected me and used this traumatic experience to continue His work in my parents' lives, as well as in mine. I know, as Paul said in Romans 8:28-29, *"that in all things God works for the good of those who love him, who have been called according to his purpose...to be conformed to the likeness of his Son."*

The prophet Jeremiah was known as the weeping prophet. His assignment was not an easy one. What God called him to proclaim was not popular with the people. Not only did they ridicule him, they did everything short of lynching him.

Why did they treat him this way? Because he was telling them that God's judgment was impending, and they needed to heed his warning. They had turned so far away from their God that, for them, right was wrong and wrong was right. They couldn't or wouldn't correct their wayward ways.

In time, God did what Jeremiah had predicted. The city of Jerusalem lay wasted, smoldering from the total destruction wreaked on it by the armies of Nebuchadnezar. As Jeremiah looked over the ruins he wept. They had received a just reward, but Jeremiah didn't gloat over the fact that what he had prophesied came to pass. He wept over the city and the people.

> *"Arise, cry out in the night as the watches of the night begin; pour out your heart like water in the presence of*

the Lord. Lift up your hands to him for the lives of your children, who faint from hunger at the head of every street. "(Lamentations 2:19)

Then, after crying and pouring out their hearts to God through the night watches Jeremiah encourages them with God's answer, even while they were still surrounded by all the devastation. Listen to his well known words in Lamentations 3:22, *"Because of the Lord's great love we are not consumed, for his compassions never fail. They are new every morning; great is your faithfulness."*

True faith perseveres. There are times when you need to set a time in the night to seek God and pour out your heart to him. He might not give you light during those times. But when you awake the next morning, believe that God has given you another day. Believe that His compassions are new and available to you. Trust in God's faithfulness, even though your circumstances haven't changed. Persevere in faith.

Samuel was another man of God often caught in the crossfire of proclaiming God's message to people who didn't follow it. One such incident took place when Samuel had to pronounce God's judgment on Saul for his disobedience. He had anointed Saul as Israel's first king. Saul made a good start, but soon began compromising his walk. God gave him clear instructions through Samuel as to how he was to deal with the Amalekites (see 1 Samuel 15). Saul didn't follow the instructions. When God told Samuel about this it says in verse 11, *"Samuel was troubled, and he cried out to the Lord all that night."* This gave him light and boldness for delivering his message of God's judgment to King Saul the next day.

When you are overwhelmed with the responsibility of confronting an obstinate, rebellious person, it is always wise to seek God and persevere in prayer, even if the burden weighs on you into the night, until courage is restored. Then go forth with confidence and confront with conviction and compassion. Leave the results with God.

Nehemiah cried out to God day and night when he heard that those who had survived the exile and were back in the land of Israel were in great trouble and disgrace. The wall of Jerusalem was broken down, and its gates had been burned. *"When I heard these things, I sat down and wept. For some days I mourned and fasted and prayed before the God of heaven."* He cried out to God, asking him to let His ear be attentive and His eyes open to hear the prayer His servant was praying before Him day and night for the people of Israel (Nehemiah 1:3-11).

These were cries of the heart for others as they faced the destructive consequences of their sins. They were also cries for wisdom in knowing how to respond to these tragic situations. As Nehemiah prayed this prayer for four long months God was giving him light. He was thinking and rethinking about what he could do in Jerusalem if he only had the opportunity.

When the king gave him a window of opportunity he was ready to buy up the opportunity. He had a plan and knew what it would take to accomplish it. He was clear in his request for help from the king. Three days after he got to Jerusalem he spent the night surveying the city to see if his plans were workable. And when he concluded that they were, he challenged the people to begin the work of rebuilding the wall around Jerusalem. He had clear job descriptions for everyone. And when the enemy reared its head he prayed and persisted in encouraging the people. To the amazement of everyone, especially Israel's enemies, they completed the project in 52 days!

Nehemiah's prevailing prayer was similar to the agonizing cries of John Knox of Scotland who prayed, "O God, give me Scotland else I die!"

Charles Finney describes John Knox in his book, *Revival of Religion.* "John Knox was a man famous for his power in prayer, so that Queen Mary of England used to say that she feared his prayers more than all the armies of Europe. And events showed that she had reason...He used to be in such an agony for the deliverance of his country, that he could not sleep. He had a place in his garden where he used to go to pray. One night he and several friends were praying together, and as they prayed, Knox spoke and said that deliverance had come. He could not tell what had happened, but he felt that something had taken place, for God had heard their prayers. What was it? Why the next news they had was that Mary was dead!"

There are others, who, like King David, were gripped with cries of the heart as they dealt with personal sins and their consequences. He shares in Psalm 32:3-7:

"When I kept silent, my bones wasted away through my groaning all day long. For day and night your hand was heavy upon me; my strength was sapped as in the heat of summer. Then I acknowledged my sin to you and did not cover up my iniquity. I said, 'I will confess my transgressions to the Lord' – and you forgave the guilt of my sin. Therefore let everyone who is godly pray to you while you may be found; surely when the mighty waters rise, they will not reach him. You are my hiding place; you will protect me from trouble and surround me with songs of deliverance."

Once being forgiven himself, he faced another consequence of his sin. Bathsheba bore him a son, but *"the Lord struck the child that Uriah's wife had borne to David, and he became ill. David pleaded with God for the child to live. He fasted and went into his house and spent the nights lying on the ground"* (2 Samuel 12:15-16). The answer he got was not what he was asking for, but it did provide light in the night for living in the day.

The boy died.

The servants were afraid to tell him. They thought David might lose his mind through his grief. But when he asked them they told him, *"Yes, he is dead."*

> *"Then David got up from the ground. After he had washed, put on lotions and changed his clothes, he went into the house of the Lord and worshiped. Then he went to his own house, and at his request they served him food, and he ate. His servants asked him, 'Why are you acting this way? While the child was alive, you fasted and wept, but now that the child is dead, you get up and eat!' He answered, 'While the child was still alive, I fasted and wept. I thought, "Who knows? The Lord may be gracious to me and let the child live." But now that he is dead, why should I fast? Can I bring him back again? I will go to him, but he will not return to me'"* (2 Samuel 12:20-23)

No one else seemed to understand. He knew where his son was – heaven. And he was confident that one day he would follow his son there. With this light he comforted his wife Bathsheba and began living for God again as the king of Israel.

More recently, Chuck Colson, the notorious White House advisor to President Nixon, experienced what the psalmist shared in Psalm 77:1-2,

> *"I cried out to God for help; I cried out to God to hear me. When I was in distress, I sought the Lord; at night I*

stretched out untiring hands and my soul refused to be comforted."

Colson's nighttime experience followed an evening at the home of Tom Phillips, president of Raytheon. In their business conversations Tom sensed Colson's need and invited him to his home for dinner. During the evening he shared his testimony and read to him from *Mere Christianity*, C.S. Lewis' cogent work on the essence of faith. What Lewis wrote about pride hit home so powerfully, Colson later wrote that it was like a torpedo had "hit me amidship."

Tom offered to pray with him, but he demurred.

After that penetrating conversation Colson left Tom's home with a copy of *Mere Christianity*. But he didn't get very far before his firm control of his emotions melted. Tears filled his eyes as he got in his car. Fumbling to find the key to start his car he mumbled to himself, "What kind of weakness is this?"

Tears overcame him as he sat in his car with the motor idling. Confused, he turned the motor off and began to get out of his car. He felt compelled to go back to the house and ask Tom to pray with him, but as he turned toward the house he saw that lights were being turned off. Through a window he saw Tom and his wife Gert make their way up the stairs to go to bed. Frozen, feeling very much alone, he realized it was too late.

When he got back into the car and drove away tears again filled his eyes, and he began sobbing uncontrollably. Not far down the road he pulled over, and in the darkness just let the tears flow. He was experiencing being broken and humbled, yet at the same time there was relief. He felt an inner cleansing and a calming of all the turmoil that had filled his mind and heart.

It was then that he prayed his first real prayer. "God, I don't know how to find You, but I'm going to try! I'm not much the way

I am now, but somehow I want to give myself to You." Then, not knowing what else to say he began repeating a prayer to God, "Take me."

Being analytical he was not sure what, if anything, had really happened. He didn't know enough to understand, to truly believe. But he had taken his first step. Alone, in the darkness of that night the light was beginning to shine. He lingered there in the light as he gradually realized he was not alone.

Not long after the cry of his heart to God, Colson took the light he had received that night and started on his journey. He went to the coast of Maine for vacation and began to read the book Tom had given him. By the end of that week God brought him to the place where he prayed what he couldn't articulate before, "Lord Jesus, I believe You. I accept You. Please come into my life. I commit it to You." Suddenly, there was a sureness in his mind that corresponded to the emotions he had felt earlier.

This was the beginning of a life-transforming experience. After spending some time in prison, himself, he began the ministry of Prison Fellowship. This catapulted him into being a crusader for justice and prison reform. He began proclaiming to all who would listen the need for a personal relationship with Jesus Christ. Many books and articles have followed.

Colson often preaches in prisons. One Christmas he was in a women's prison in North Carolina. After his message he was asked if he would be willing personally to visit a prisoner, Bessie Shipp, who was in solitary confinement. When he agreed an official cautioned him, "She has AIDS."

At first he tried thinking of an excuse for not going in to see Bessie, but then he remembered seeing Mother Teresa on television. She was sharing how AIDS victims need to hear about God's love. This emboldened him to go ahead with visiting this lonely, dying prisoner. Before the visit was over, gently holding her cold hands, he prayed with Bessie as she received Jesus Christ as her Savior. Three weeks later she died.

Charles Colson not only received justice in his life, but also became a crusader for justice on behalf of the underprivileged and unrepresented. His experience has provided light in the night for living in the day for many of his readers, listeners, and benefactors.

The Bible lists many accounts where individuals cried out to God because they were burdened for someone else in dire need. Others cried out to God because they personally were facing overwhelming circumstances. Often this happened at night. Ordinary people and prominent people found that when they faced staggering odds, one final option was to cry out to God. When they did they found that God is faithful to keep His promise to answer the cries of the heart and give His peace.

Application Questions:
1. Of the people described in this chapter who cried out to God in the night, which one do you identify with most?
2. Was what happened to you and your response something that happened spontaneously or was it more intentional?
3. How has God responded to your cry?
4. What outcomes have taken place as a result of your experience?

Suggested Prayer:
"Dear heavenly Father, though the experience I had (or am going through now) was not easy to go through, I want to thank you for it, because it has brought me to realize how much I need you. Thank You for being there whenever I need You and for listening to the cry of my heart. Thank You for healing me and helping me go on in the light You have shown me. In Christ's name, Amen"

Lud Golz

Chapter Six

Promises to Live By: Can I Count on Your Promise God?

"Last night an angel of the God whose I am and whom I serve stood beside me and said, 'Do not be afraid, Paul. You must stand trial before Caesar; and God has graciously given you the lives of all who sail with you.' So keep up your courage, men, for I have faith in God that it will happen just as He told me." (Acts 27:23-25)

Paul, on his way to Rome as a prisoner, was on a boat that was viciously tossed by the relentless wind and waves. He had warned the crew and his Roman guard that this would likely happen if they continued the voyage from Crete. The majority on board wanted to continue.

At first the winds seemed cooperative, but out of nowhere a northeast wind of hurricane force swept down from the island. Conditions worsened. When all hope was gone, Paul received a promise from God during the night.

The next day he shared it with all on board.

"Men, you should have taken my advice not to sail from Crete; then you would have spared yourselves this damage and loss. But now I urge you to keep up your courage, because not one of you will be lost; only the ship will be destroyed. Last night an angel of the God whose I am and whom I serve stood beside me and said, 'Do not be afraid, Paul. You must stand trial before Caesar; and God has graciously given you the lives of all who sail with you.' So keep up your courage, men, for I have faith in God that it will happen just as he told me."

He had received a promise to live by and as a result was able to instruct all on board what to do and assure them that if they followed his instructions all would get safely to shore. That is the power of a promise to live by.

In an earlier chapter we discovered that God gave a promise to Abraham one night. As you read the history of his life, it was obvious Abraham did not always live in the light of that night's promise. But the promise was like the magnetic pole that enables the compass to work, ultimately keeping your life on target. Time and again he was drawn back into alignment with God's promised plan. Even when God asked him to offer up his son Isaac as a sacrifice, faith in the promise enabled him to obey God. He was convinced that in the light of the promise God could and would raise him from the dead if necessary (Hebrews 11:17-19).

God repeated the promise to Abraham's son, Isaac, when he was at Beersheba.

"That night the Lord appeared to him and said, 'I am the God of your father Abraham. Do not be afraid, for I am with you; I will bless you and will increase the number of

your descendants for the sake of my servant Abraham.'"
(Genesis 26:24)

Did you notice? This happened at night!
We've already considered when and where God repeated the promise to Jacob. As he fled from his brother Esau, he had the dream one night of the ladder that reached up to heaven. From above the ladder God repeated the promise (Genesis 28:10-22).

In Genesis 46:1-4 God once more repeated the promise to Jacob, now called Israel.

> *"So Israel set out with all that was his, and when he reached Beersheba, he offered sacrifices to the God of his father Isaac. And God spoke to Israel in a vision at night and said, 'Jacob! Jacob!' 'Here I am,' he replied. 'I am God, the God of your father,' he said. 'Do not be afraid to go down to Egypt, for I will make you into a great nation there. I will go down to Egypt with you, and I will surely bring you back again. And Joseph's own hand will close your eyes.'"*

Time and again these patriarchs received light in the night for living in the day! And though they didn't always follow the light of the promise wholeheartedly, they were drawn forward by it. The promise for them was what it says in Psalm 119:105, *"Your word is a lamp to my feet and a light for my path."*

The story of Ruth in the Old Testament develops as a result of the promise of a kinsman-redeemer. Elimilech, his wife Naomi and their two sons moved to Moab because of a famine in their land. While in Moab, Elimilech died. The two sons married Moabite women. One of them was Ruth. Shortly after that both sons died.

Naomi heard that the famine was over in her homeland and decided to return. She felt that it would be best for her daughters-in-law to remain in their own land where they could most likely find new husbands. Ruth refused that option, having come to know and appreciate the God of Israel. She determined to return with Naomi so she could be with her new extended family and worship its God.

When they arrived their situation was quite difficult. To help out Ruth went out into the fields to glean leftover grain left behind by the harvesters. She happened to glean in a field owned by Boaz, one of Naomi's relatives. He immediately noticed her when he arrived and asked his foreman who she was. When he said, *"She is the Moabitess who came back from Moab with Naomi,"* Boaz perked up. He had heard some positive things about her. He showed her favor and encouraged her to continue working in his fields.

When Naomi, Ruth's mother-in-law, saw the favor Boaz was showing toward Ruth, she began developing a plan that was based on the provision of a kinsman-redeemer. This provision meant that it was the duty of a kinsman to redeem the paternal estate which his nearest relative lost, and also to marry a deceased kinsman's widow.

At the time when they were winnowing barley on the threshing floor, she thought it would be appropriate for Ruth to take the initiative and let Boaz know she was interested in him becoming her kinsman-redeemer. She followed the detailed plan of Naomi to a "T."

That night she prepared herself to be most desirable.

"When Boaz had finished eating and drinking and was in good spirits, he went over to lie down at the far end of the grain pile. Ruth approached quietly, uncovered his feet

and lay down. In the middle of the night something startled the man, and he turned and discovered a woman lying at his feet. 'Who are you?' he asked. 'I am your servant Ruth' she said. 'Spread the corner of your garment over me, since you are a kinsman-redeemer.'"
(Ruth 3:7-9)

Boaz was impressed with Ruth the moment he laid eyes on her. He was interested in her but did nothing about it other than show her favor by encouraging her to work with his girls in the field. When he received light in the night on that threshing floor, his heart skipped a beat. He promised to live out in the day what he had learned in the night.

"The Lord bless you, my daughter," he said. "This kindness is greater than that which you showed earlier: You have not run after the younger men, whether rich or poor. And now, my daughter, don't be afraid. I will do for you all you ask. All my fellow townsmen know that you are a woman of noble character. Although it is true that I am near of kin, there is a kinsman-redeemer nearer than I. Stay here for the night, and in the morning if he wants to redeem, good; let him redeem. But if he is not willing, as surely as the Lord lives I will do it." (Ruth 3:10-13)

In the morning he followed all the appropriate protocol in order to find out if he would be able to become Ruth's kinsman-redeemer. When it was clear that he was free to marry her, he did. The result of this light in the night that he lived out in the day was the birth of Obed. He was the father of Jesse, the father of David.

This was the line of promise that ultimately led to the birth of our Savior, Jesus Christ!

Throughout the years I often found myself in difficult circumstances as I endeavored to carry out what I believed God called me to do. I had restless nights where I got up and went to a room in the house where I would not disturb anyone. I would either sit in the quietness or walk back and forth or fall on my knees as I sought God for light. Often the only light was the reminder of the promise, *"Surely I am with you always, to the very end of the age."* (Matthew 28:20)

During the summer after my first year in college, I was on a mission trip to Venezuela. God provided enough money for me to fly there and return to America, plus a little to live on. Most of the trip was with a missionary pilot who flew us down the Caribbean chain of islands. When I got to Venezuela, I put $115 aside, the amount needed for the return flight to America.

One night, early that summer, as I was praying for Amado Chanco, a national worker in the Philippines, I got the impression that God wanted me to send him $25. I was getting by with the little money I had by eating cereal for breakfast and peanut butter sandwiches and bananas the rest of the time. Occasionally, I was invited out for dinner which provided some balance in my diet.

As the impression to send the $25 grew in my mind and heart, I argued with God in prayer, "I'm hardly able to scrape by with the money I have to live on. I'm certainly not going to touch the money I laid aside for the trip back to America.!"

God countered by reminding me that He provided the money for this trip. In reality, it was His money, not mine.

Finally, I decided to trust Him to keep His promise to meet all my needs according to His glorious riches in Christ Jesus (Philippians 4:19). I sat down and wrote a brief note to Amado Chanco and put in the $25 from the amount I had set aside for my trip home. I quickly sealed the envelope before I could change my mind. Then, first thing the next morning, I sent it off. This light in the night for living in the day stretched my faith as the summer wore on.

When the time for returning to America approached, I still was short of money for the return flight because of the $25 gift I made earlier that summer. I began to feel that God might want me to stay in Venezuela. I talked about my predicament with some missionaries who had befriended me. When they learned of my situation they invited me to join them in their interior jungle post. This option excited me. Immediately I started making plans to do that.

Then, on the final day before a two-week outreach trip, just before those who had come for the conference would return to America, I was in a discussion with a number of men. One, who had a ticket for the flight back to America, said, "I'd like to extend my time in South America by going on to Ecuador. I've checked it out and it would cost me an extra $75 to do that. Do any of you know someone who would be interested in buying my return ticket for $75?"

When he said that my heart started racing and my mind buzzed with questions. Finally, I acknowledged, "I'm interested, but first I need to pray about it." Then, I asked him, "Could I get back to you tomorrow morning?" He agreed, so I took the bus to where I was staying and determined to stay up that night until I got an answer from God.

I prayed. I read the Bible. I prayed. I sat still and waited for an answer. Nothing. My mind drew a total blank. I didn't know if I should follow through on the plans to stay with the missionaries or to cancel those plans and buy the ticket home to America. After a long time of wrestling and still drawing a blank, I capitulated to my body's weariness, thinking it might be wise to get some rest and pursue it further early the next morning. I promptly fell asleep and rested well till early morning.

Again I started praying, reading, waiting, listening…Nothing! I knew I needed to come up with an answer in a couple of hours. What was I to do? Finally a thought came to me. I took out a piece of paper and on one side wrote across the top, RETURN. Under that I drew a line down the middle of the page. On the left side I wrote down all the reasons I could think of for returning to America. On the right side I wrote down all the reasons for not returning. On the backside I did the same under the heading, STAY. After totaling and then reviewing all the *pros* and *cons,* for RETURN and for STAY, I determined that I should return to America and continue my education at Moody Bible Institute in Chicago.

I had no inner impression drawing me either way, so I prayed to God, "I'm going to go and buy the ticket for $75. If You want me to stay, You have to stop me." I didn't know how God might do that, but I got ready, took the bus to where the group was meeting and bought the ticket. God didn't stop me, so I changed my plans from staying and working with the missionaries in Venezuela's jungles and prepared to return to America. I went to Moody and further prepared to serve God.

I had put $115 aside for the trip home, but actually got the ticket for $75. By sending the $25 to the national worker in the Philippines I actually ended up with an extra $15! God kept His promise to meet all my needs and then some.

My decision to return to America was not a dramatic experience. It was rather agonizing. But the light I received was to surrender myself to God, pray for guidance and then use the mind God had given me. Preferably you should take more time to work through this process than I did, but on that occasion I didn't have more time.

During the years I've refined the process. Now, when facing an important decision, I recommend trying to find biblical support for as many of the *pros* and *cons* as possible. Look especially for promises that God has given in His word. Also, seek the counsel of others in whom you have confidence. This is what Paul's prayer articulated in Colossians 1:9, *"We have not stopped praying for you and asking God to fill you with the knowledge of his will through all spiritual wisdom and understanding."* Use your mind and seek spiritual discernment to determine clearly what God's will is. Then, just do it!

I believe that most of the time men like Paul the Apostle made decisions this way. Every once in a while, however, God gave them special light in the night for living in the day. An example would be the promise God gave Paul when he was in Corinth.

"One night the Lord spoke to Paul in a vision: 'Do not be afraid; keep on speaking, do not be silent. For I am with you, and no one is going to attack and harm you, because I have many people in this city.' So, Paul stayed for a year and a half, teaching them the word of God." (Acts 18:9-11)

All who genuinely seek to do the will of God will at times be confronted with tough decisions. Some times we get ourselves into those situations by our own previous choices. At other times others make decisions that complicate our lives. Then there are situations that develop over which we and others have no control. Whatever the case, if we want to know and do God's will, there are steps we can take. Prayerfully use your head to think through the options. Ask God for wisdom to discern what He wants us to see. Seek the counsel of others. Most important, search the Bible for promises you can count on as you step out in obedience to what you believe is God's will. Then trust God to order your steps. He said He would in Proverbs 16:9, *"In his heart a man plans his course, but the Lord determines his steps."*

Application Questions:
1. What is your favorite promise in the Bible?
2. Has God used a promise to help you get through a difficult time in your life?
3. Have you ever used the decision making procedure described in this chapter?
4. Are you facing a difficult decision in your life now? Why not try using it?
5. Can you think of a promise that applies to your situation?

Suggested Prayer:
"Dear God, I need your insight and help as I wrestle with this decision. As Paul prayed for the Colossian Christians, fill me with the knowledge of Your will through all spiritual wisdom and understanding. Help me to use my mind and give me the ability to discern your will. Remind me of a promise You have given in Your Word and enable me to trust You to fulfill it as I seek to do your will. In Christ's name, Amen."

Chapter Seven

I Don't Understand: Can You Help Me God?

"I will praise the Lord, who counsels me; even at night my heart instructs me. I have set the Lord always before me. Because he is at my right hand, I will not be shaken." (Psalm 16:7)

I will never forget an experience Mur and I had while on a trip to Africa to visit with two couples our church helped to support in the work they were doing there. One couple was in Nigeria and the other in Chad. While traveling in Africa it is almost impossible to get flights from one country to another by going either East or West. You have to fly North or South and kind of zig-zag to get there.

We found a cheaper way by hiring a missionary pilot who would fly directly east from Nigeria to Chad. Once in Fort Lamy, he would take us to the southern region of Chad to visit the other couple.

When our first visit was over, we were scheduled to leave for Chad the next morning. But during the night an African dust storm, called a harmattan, blew in. The pilot informed us that we couldn't leave that day. We would have to wait out the storm.

Fortunately, we were able to leave the following morning, even though there was still a fair amount of dust to fly through until our altitude reached over 4,000 feet. The trip went without incident. After we landed, the pilot informed us that he would not be able to take us south to see our friends. He said the plane was scheduled for a check up, and he couldn't take us there until that was done.

Our first reaction was frustration. Our arrangements were made some time prior to our coming and they had agreed to take us all the way. But there was nothing we could do about it. We looked into going south another way, but everything seemed to be unworkable. We even found the American embassy people indifferent and unhelpful. Finally, we called the couple to see what they would counsel us. They said that, unfortunately, though disappointed, it would probably be wise to cancel our visit.

On top of this, the weather was unbearable -- 110 degrees Fahrenheit, dry and dusty. And to make matters worse, virtually no one spoke English. Since we planned to stay with our friends for six days, we were stuck in this very undesirable place.

When we called the airline to confirm our tickets for the next flight, we found that our reservation for leaving Chad on 2/6 (which we in the US understand as February 6), was interpreted by our airline as the second day of June! There was no room on the flight on which we thought we had a reservation. Muslims were traveling to Mecca in droves to fulfill their religious pilgrimage obligations. Another problem was that we needed a transit visa to go through Sudan on our way to Egypt. Our travel agent had missed that. Even if we got on our flight as planned, they would not let us fly without the visa!

I clearly remember one night lying under a mosquito net, clammy with sweat and restless in spirit. I was praying -- NO! -- complaining to God for the umpteenth time, "God, I don't understand this. Mur and I are here to serve and encourage our friends and we can't even get to them. We're stuck here in this forsaken place. No one cares about our situation. We don't even know if we can get out of here. And we have spent a lot of money that people have graciously given to make all this possible. We're wasting time and money."

As I was ranting and raving in my mind and heart, God reminded me of Paul and his travels. He, too, struggled with frustration at times. Listen to what he wrote about his suffering in 2 Corinthians 11:23-27:

> *"Are they servants of Christ? (I am out of my mind to talk like this.) I am more. I have worked much harder, been in prison more frequently, been flogged more severely, and been exposed to death again and again. Five times I received from the Jews the forty lashes minus one. Three times I was beaten with rods, once I was stoned, three times I was shipwrecked, I spent a night and a day in the open sea, I have been constantly on the move. I have been in danger from rivers, in danger from bandits, in danger from my own countrymen, in danger from Gentiles; in danger in the city, in danger in the country, in danger at sea; and in danger from false brothers. I have labored and toiled and have often gone without sleep; I have known hunger and thirst and have often gone without food; I have been cold and naked."*

No, I wasn't reading this. Everything was dark. It was quiet, except for the reminder of the mosquito nets that kept out those buzzing creatures that would love to make me even more uncomfortable. No, I was just reminded of the fact that Paul had gone through much more than we were going through. I seemed to hear God say to me,

> *"Who do you think you are? Are you on a more important journey than Paul was on as he went from place to place? And what about Jesus who once said, 'Foxes have holes and birds of the air have nests, but the Son of Man has no place to lay his head.'"*
> (Matthew 8:20)

All of a sudden I perceived light in the night. God provided the light, but He used scriptures I had studied and some I had memorized. They were a part of my mental data base, a truth reservoir, from which God could provide insight. And in the days that followed, God helped me to experience the practicality of that light. Paul put it this way in Philippians 4:11-13,

> *"I have learned to be content whatever the circumstances. I know what it is to be in need, and I know what it is to have plenty. I have learned the secret of being content in any and every situation, whether well fed or hungry, whether living in plenty or in want. I can do everything through him who gives me strength"*

The next couple of days in Fort Lamy were tough. When Sunday arrived we decided to go to church. We couldn't understand what was being said. The songs were unfamiliar. But we were able to participate meaningfully in their communion service. The symbolism in communion crosses language barriers.

After church a man came up to us and asked, "Didn't I see you in the embassy the other day?" We told him that we, indeed, had been there. It was good to talk to someone who spoke American

English and seemed genuinely to care for us and our situation. He asked us if we would like to come to his home for Sunday dinner. We gladly accepted.

While enjoying an American, home cooked meal, our host told us he would try to help us work out our travel problems. The next day we went to the Sudan embassy to get a transit visa application. Then he helped us find a photographer to take pictures for the visa. We filled out all the papers and delivered them to the embassy and then planned to pray, hoping they would be processed in time for the flight. He also helped us with the airline to get our reservations switched to 6/2, that is, the sixth day of February!

As we waited for our visas to be processed, we found out that there was a commercial airline that flew to where our friends, Bill and Nancy Francis, were serving. They flew there one day and back the next, within the time we were in the country. We prayed about it and decided to go for it. But we didn't call Bill and Nancy, hoping to surprise them.

On the flight down we met some Peace Corps workers. They were being picked up by fellow Peace Corps workers who agreed to take us to where Bill and Nancy lived. When we got to their compound, some workers told us that they were in town shopping. So, we continued downtown and drove around until we found Bill and Nancy. They were surprised and befuddled to see us!

What a memorable visit, though brief. They were so appreciative of our effort to see them that as we were getting ready to board the flight back to Fort Lamy, Bill pushed something into my pocket. I was carrying our luggage so I couldn't feel what it was until we were in our seats and taxiing toward the runway. It was a roll of money with a note: "We have been saving for a vacation. We will postpone it. This is to help with your extra expenses. Your visit really touched us. Love, Bill and Nancy."

We appreciated their thoughtfulness so much but didn't want to keep the money. What to do? Fortunately, when we got to Fort Lamy, we met a missionary who was flying back the next day to Bill and Nancy's town. We gave the money to her and asked her to take it back to them. What a wonderful memory the visit was for both them and us.

We got back early enough to pick up our pictures, take them to the embassy and get our visas so we could continue our journey without any further delay.

Though there were further complications on that same trip, God gave us the peace and contentment Paul talked about. Our flight out of Egypt was canceled. This meant we had to go to Cyprus, via Lebanon. By the time we got to Cyprus the next day, we missed our flight to Israel. This cut our planned time in Israel down to just three days. But God helped us see most of what we had planned in those few days.

Mur was heading home from Israel and I was going further east to Sri Lanka. She left early on Valentine's Day. It was hard parting because I would be traveling for another six weeks before returning home. After seeing her off, I went back to the hotel and relaxed some before returning to the airport in the afternoon for my flight to India and Sri Lanka.

While sitting in the waiting area I took some time to read my Bible. A teenager from Thailand walked up to me and inquired, "Are you reading the Bible"

"Yes," I replied.

She asked, "Could I talk to you?"

I had plenty of time before my flight, so I agreed.

She was an exchange student during the past year and was returning home to Bankok. While in America she lived with a Christian family and went to church with them. After learning about Jesus Christ, she made a life changing decision. She prayed to receive Him as her Savior. Now she was returning to her Buddhist family in Thailand and she was feeling afraid of what they were going to think about her new found faith in Christ.

I felt as though I was reliving the experience Phillip the evangelist had, described in Acts 8:26-39. He was led by the Holy Spirit to go to the desert road leading from Jerusalem to Gaza. There he met an Ethiopian eunuch, an important official in charge of the treasury of Candace, queen of the Ethiopians. He had gone to Jerusalem to worship and now, on his way home, was sitting in his chariot reading the book of Isaiah the prophet. Phillip asked him, *"Do you understand what you are reading?"*

"How can I unless someone explains it to me?' he replied. Then he turned to Philip and asked him if he would come up and sit with him in his chariot. Then he asked him, *"Tell me, please, who is the prophet talking abut, himself or someone else?"*

Philip used the very passage he was reading to launch into an explanation of the good news about Jesus.

Before Philip was through the eunuch asked to be baptized as a believer in Jesus Christ. As he continued on his journey he was filled with joy, because now he knew in a personal way the one he had tried worshipping in a superficial way before.

As I talked to this Tai teenager, I became aware of the time slipping away. I asked her when her flight was scheduled to depart. To my surprise it was the same time as mine. As we looked into it further, we discovered we were on the same flight! We decided to see if we could sit together. Amazingly, we were able to arrange sitting together all the way to Bombay, and then on to Sri Lanka.

We had all night to talk about her relationship with Jesus Christ, her understanding of the Bible, her concerns about sharing her new life with her family and how she might respond to their questions. What a unique experience to share with her light in the night for living in the day. Only God knows how important that time was that He had arranged for her. To her credit, she was wise enough to seek help. She didn't know much about her new found faith, but she knew it was based on the Bible. That's why she came to me, a total stranger, because I was reading the Bible, something we had in common.

A paraphrase of Psalm 112:4-7 might read,

*"Even in darkness light dawns for the upright, for the gracious and compassionate and righteous **girl**...surely **she** will never be shaken; a righteous **girl** will be remembered forever. **She** will have no fear of bad news; **her** heart is steadfast, trusting in the Lord." (bold added)*

Nicodemus also sought help from someone he trusted. He came to Jesus at night, searching for truth (John 3:1-15). He, too, received light in the night for living in the day. He was introduced to the wonderful truth of being born again, or from above, by the Spirit of God. This is an experience made possible by a provision explained by Jesus in those well-known verses of John 3:16-21,

"For God so loved the world that he gave his one and only Son, that whoever believes in him shall not perish but have eternal life. For God did not send his Son into the world to condemn the world, but to save the world through him. Whoever believes in him is not condemned...whoever lives by the truth comes into the light, so that it may be seen plainly that what he has done has been done through God."

I believe Nicodemus made that decision, and his life was never the same. At first, he kept his attraction to Jesus a secret. Then, when Jesus was being falsely accused by his fellow religious leaders he spoke up and asked, *"Does our law condemn anyone without first hearing him to find out what he is doing?"*

Their reply was predictable. Avoiding the legitimate question, they attacked Nicodemus,

> *"Are you from Galilee, too? Look into it, and you will find that a prophet does not come out of Galilee."* (John 7:50-52)

Later, at the death of Christ, he went public even more by joining Joseph of Arimathea in taking Christ's body down from the cross and placing it in Joseph's almost-finished tomb (John 19:38-42). Once you enter into a personal relationship with Jesus Christ and experience this new life He offers, you can't keep it to yourself, hidden from others. You find yourself compelled gradually to let the light you have received shine before others.

As people who have trusted in Jesus Christ continue to grow in their faith, they will discover what Jesus said to His disciples in Acts 1:8,

> *"But you will receive power when the Holy Spirit comes on you; and you will be my witnesses'* (The William's translation reads, *'you must be my witnesses')* *in Jerusalem, and in all Judea and Samaria, and to the ends of the earth."*

Read the book of Acts and you will discover that this is precisely what happened during the months and years that followed.

It always amazes me to see how God allows us to face a crisis in order to teach us something we would have a hard time learning or understanding in a classroom. That's one reason He included in the Bible experiences similar to ones we face. Paul says in 1 Corinthians 10:1-13, that we should learn from their experiences and when we face similar situations remember and apply what we have learned. If we don't learn from them and remember the lessons, God will teach us the hard way. If, on the other hand, we are uninformed or immature, God is gracious and patient in providing help. He often will bring someone into our lives who can counsel and encourage us. He wants us to be wise and provides what we need to become wise. Our responsibility is to listen, observe, receive and apply what He provides.

Application Questions:
1. Have you ever experienced God arranging things so that you received insight in the night to understand better your circumstances and how to cope with them?
2. When that happened, did God use scripture that you had studied or memorized?
3. In what ways has that insight helped you to cope with the situation you were facing or with situations you have faced since then?
4. Has God ever brought someone into your life who provided insight to help you get through a tough time?
5. Did you take time to thank God? Did you ever write a thank you note to the one God used to give you insight?

Suggested Prayer:
"Dear, loving Father. Thank you for the times you have provided insight and understanding for me to better cope with the situations I was facing. Thank you also for _____, whom you sent to me at a critical time to give insight into questions I had and situations I was struggling with. You have been faithful. Thank you. In Jesus name, Amen."

Chapter Eight

Protection and Deliverance: Is it Safe to Go On?

"The following night the Lord stood near Paul and said, 'Take courage! As you have testified about me in Jerusalem, so you must also testify in Rome.'" (Acts 23:11)

One of the clearest dynamics demonstrated throughout the Bible is how God protects and delivers His people so His purpose will be fulfilled. Often that protection and deliverance takes place during the night.

It was during the night that God used Abraham to rescue Lot who had been taken captive by enemies with all his family and possessions (Genesis 14:15). The exodus from Egypt started during the fateful night when all the firstborn died throughout Egypt in the homes where the doorposts had not been brushed with blood (Exodus 12:21-30).

Later, God set the stage for the great deliverance of the Israelites as they crossed the Red Sea. When the Israelites got to the Red Sea and saw the Egyptian army approaching they were terrified. They were boxed in. Feeling helpless they cried out to God. Then they complained to Moses for getting them into this hopeless predicament.

There are times when we are to roll up our sleeves and tackle whatever needs to be done. As we do this, however, we need to trust in God to give strength and guidance. But there are other times when God says, *"Do not be afraid. Stand firm, and you will see the deliverance the Lord will bring you."* When that happens, don't try to help God do what He says He will do. You'll only get in the way. Just trust, watch and follow His lead. That's precisely what Moses said to the complaining, fearful Israelites.

> *"Do not be afraid. Stand firm and you will see the deliverance the Lord will bring you today. The Egyptians you see today you will never see again. The Lord will fight for you; you need only to be still."*
> (Exodus 14:13-14)

God's presence seen in the pillar of cloud that was in front of the people moved and stood behind them, coming between the Egyptian army and the people of Israel. Throughout the night the cloud brought darkness to the one side and light to the other side; so neither went near the other all night long.

> *"Then Moses stretched out his hand over the sea, and all that night the Lord drove the sea back with a strong east wind and turned it into dry land. The waters were divided, and the Israelites went through the sea on dry ground...The Egyptians pursued them...During the last watch of the night the Lord looked down from the pillar of fire and cloud at the Egyptian army and threw it into confusion...Then the Lord said to Moses, 'Stretch out your hand over the sea so that the waters may flow back over the Egyptians and their chariots and horsemen.' Moses stretched out his hand over the*

sea, and at daybreak the sea went back to its place...The water flowed back and covered the chariots and horsemen – the entire army of Pharaoh that had followed the Israelites into the sea. Not one of them survived...when the Israelites saw the great power the Lord displayed against the Egyptians, the people feared the Lord and put their trust in him and in Moses his servant. " (Exodus 14:26-29)

This experience of deliverance from Egypt was to be commemorated annually during the Passover celebration so the Jews would never forget God's mighty power to protect and deliver. It was to be light in the night for living in the day throughout the years ahead.

Gideon and his "fleece test" to determine whether or not God really wanted him to go to battle against the Midianites is well known. It was during the night that God, in answer to Gideon's request, caused the fleece to have dew on it with everything around it remaining dry. The second night Gideon asked the opposite, that the fleece stay dry while dew would be on everything around it. God granted that as well.

This prepared Gideon to gather an army to fight against the Midianites. But God wanted Gideon to trust in Him, not in his army. He gave him specific instructions as to how he was to trim the army to just 300 men.

Gideon still didn't feel quite ready to attack. He decided to sneak down to the camp of the enemy. As he approached he heard a man share a dream he had:

"...a round loaf of barley bread came tumbling into the Midianite camp. It struck the tent with such force that the tent overturned and collapsed." Then he heard a fellow

soldier interpret the dream: *"This can be nothing other than the sword of Gideon son of Joash, the Israelite. God has given the Midianites and the whole camp into his hands."* (Judges 7:13-14)

When Gideon heard this he took courage, got his men ready and attacked. He didn't even wait until daybreak to act on the light he had received from God. God protected and delivered him, his army that was significantly outnumbered and the nation of Israel.

The prophet Daniel was protected a number of times during the night. When Nebuchadnezzar had a dream that troubled him, he brought in the wise men in his kingdom. He asked them to tell him what he had dreamed and interpret it for him. They knew that they could not do what was asked and told the king that no king had ever asked for such a thing. The king was infuriated and ordered all the wise men to be executed.

"Men were sent to look for Daniel and his friends to put them to death. When Arioch, the commander of the king's guard, had gone out to put to death the wise men of Babylon, Daniel spoke to him with wisdom and tact. He asked the king's officer, 'Why did the king issue such a harsh decree?' Arioch then explained the matter to Daniel. At this, Daniel went in to the king and asked for time, so that he might interpret the dream for him. Then Daniel returned to his house and explained the matter to his friends Hanania, Mishael and Azariah. He urged them to plead for mercy from the God of heaven concerning this mystery, so that he and his friends might not be executed with the rest of the wise men of Babylon. During the night the mystery was revealed to Daniel in a vision." (Daniel 2:13-19)

Daniel knew where to find the answer to the question the king had presented. He also knew the key to getting the answer. God had the answer, and prayer was the key. He sought the support of his friends; together they prayed to God that night. Before the night was over the mystery was revealed to Daniel in a vision.

This is an Old Testament example of what Jesus taught in Matthew 18:19-20,

> *"Again, I tell you that if two of you on earth agree about anything you ask for, it will be done for you by my Father in heaven. For where two or three come together in my name, there am I with them."*

When Daniel told the king what God had revealed to him the king not only stayed the execution of the wise men, he honored Daniel by placing him *"in a high position and lavished many gifts on him. He made him ruler over the entire province of Babylon and placed him in charge of all its wise men."* (Daniel 2:48)

Daniel had another nighttime deliverance. This reinforced the light he already had about God's protection. In addition, his experience became light in the night for Darius the king. He had been tricked by his political advisors into having Daniel thrown into a den of lions. Daniel spent a night in the den of lions unharmed. When God protected Daniel from the lions, the king had Daniel restored to his position of honor. He also had the perpetrators of the scheme to get rid of Daniel thrown into the den of lions.

> *"And before they reached the floor of the den, the lions overpowered them and crushed all their bones."*
> (Daniel 6:24)

Listen to the testimony of King Darius written to all the peoples, nations and men of every language throughout the land:

"May you prosper greatly! I issue a decree that in every part of my kingdom people must fear and reverence the God of Daniel. For he is the living God and he endures forever; his kingdom will not be destroyed, his dominion will never end. He rescues and he saves; he performs signs and wonders in the heavens and on the earth. He has rescued Daniel from the power of the lions." (Daniel 6:25-27)

Darius did more than just give a testimony. He reinstated Daniel and saw to it that he prospered during the rest of his reign. And God continued to bless Daniel during the reign of Cyrus the Persian (Daniel 6:28).

When Jesus was born God protected Him from the evil designs of King Herod. After the Magi visited and worshiped Jesus, God warned them in a dream not to go back to Herod to inform him where Jesus could be found in Bethlehem. They left that same night and returned to their country by another route.

"When they had gone, an angel of the Lord appeared to Joseph in a dream. 'Get up,' he said, 'take the child and his mother and escape to Egypt. Stay there until I tell you, for Herod is going to search for the child to kill him.' So he got up, took the child and his mother during the night and left for Egypt." (Matthew 2:13-14)

Later in the same chapter you read about the holocaust King Herod ordered, killing all the boys in Bethlehem and its vicinity who were two years old and younger. Jesus was protected because Joseph acted promptly on the light he had received that night.

In Acts 5 you read about the high priest and his cohorts arresting the apostles and putting them in the public jail.

"But during the night an angel of the Lord opened the doors of the jail and brought them out. 'Go, stand in the temple courts,' he said, 'and tell the people the full message of this new life.'" (Acts 5:17-20)

Again in Acts 12 Peter was put into prison and guarded very carefully. The church earnestly prayed for him.

"The night before Herod was to bring him to trial, Peter was sleeping between two soldiers, bound with two chains, and sentries stood guard at the entrance. Suddenly an angel of the Lord appeared and a light shone in the cell. He struck Peter on the side and woke him up. 'Quick, get up!' he said, and the chains fell off Peter's wrists. Then the angel said to him, 'Put on your clothes and sandals.' And Peter did so. 'Wrap your cloak around you and follow me,' the angel told him. Peter followed him out of the prison, but he had no idea that what the angel was doing was really happening; he thought he was seeing a vision. They passed the first and second guards and came to the iron gate leading to the city. It opened for them by itself, and they went through it. When they had walked the length of one street, suddenly the angel left him. Then Peter came to himself and said, 'Now I know without a doubt that the Lord sent his angel and rescued me from Herod's clutches and from everything the Jewish people were anticipating.'" (Acts 12:6-11)

When he received this light in the night, he didn't wait until daybreak to share what had happened. He went right to the home of Mary where he knew fellow believers would be praying for him to let them know he was delivered. How did he know that they would be praying at Mary's home? That was a common practice of the believers, especially when one of them was in need. He told them to tell James and the brothers, and he went to another place to share the good news. You can imagine the rejoicing and faith building that took place among believers. Meanwhile, imagine the commotion and confusion that took place in the prison and in the King's court. In fact, when they couldn't find Peter anywhere, the soldiers who were to protect him were executed.

More examples are found throughout the book of Acts of God's protection and deliverance during the night hours. Paul escaped from Damascus by being lowered at night in a basket through an opening in the wall, because those who wanted to kill him were watching the gates of the city (Acts 9:25). He was protected and delivered from prison in Philippi (Acts 16:25-40), from threatening circumstances in Corinth (Acts 18:1-17), from a plot to kill him while being moved from a prison in Jerusalem to Caesarea (Acts 23:11-35). As a prisoner he was being transported from Caesarea to Rome. En-route they were caught in a fierce storm. Paul, though a prisoner, took charge. He shared how God had assured him during the night that all would get to shore alive. Then he gave instructions about how to prepare for the ship getting grounded and torn apart by the waves. Though the ship was destroyed not one on board lost their lives. God kept His promise (Acts 27:21-44).

All of these experiences involved receiving light in the night for living in the day. And they are recorded for our benefit. They provide encouragement and comfort as we face dangerous or trying situations. They are also faith builders.

As a teen I traveled one summer to South America to serve in a youth outreach venture. Flying from Trinidad to Venezuela, I was the only "Gringo" on the plane. After we landed at a small coastal city, we were processed through customs. A soldier on board came up to me and asked where I was going. I told him I was going to the capital city of Caracas to participate in a Christian youth congress. When he asked me how I was going to get there, I responded, "By bus."

He suggested that would not be a good idea. In broken English he explained, "Busses are old and break down. Everything is packed on board – dogs, chickens, vegetable and fruit baskets, and all kinds of packages. The smell is bad and it's very hot." He told me he was going to be going to Caracas himself in two days, and he would arrange for me to travel with him. That sounded safer, especially since I didn't speak Spanish, so I agreed.

As we walked through customs he motioned to the agent that I was with him. Since he was a soldier, serving under a dictator, they didn't argue with him. They stamped our passports and we were on our way. When we got outside he waved to a guy in a Jeep. We climbed in and he gave directions to the driver.

Within a few blocks we stopped at the house of a pastor. After explaining my mission plans for the summer he told the pastor to take care of me, said he would pick me up in two days, and left. I couldn't speak Spanish and this pastor, who was a widower, and his two daughters, couldn't speak English. I had an English/Spanish dictionary and with hand-signs and pointing to words in the dictionary we got by. It was a stretching experience for all of us, but enjoyable in spite of the awkwardness of the situation.

When the soldier didn't pick me up at the planned time, I started walking toward the office of the taxi company. On the way the soldier met me. We went to the taxi company and soon were in a car and on our way. This is how it worked. They crammed as many people into the car as possible. People entered and left the car all along the way. We traveled from noon all the way through the night until mid morning the next day.

During the night I must admit I was scared a good bit of the time, but I quietly called out to God for protection and courage. I repeated in my mind the promises of God I had memorized. They became my comfort. They became light in the night for living through the night, the next day, and for the rest of that summer.

When all the other passengers were dropped off in Caracas, the soldier directed the driver to his barracks. When he got out he gave him directions to the missionary's home. We drove for some time through narrow streets with rundown buildings on each side. Eventually we got to the home of the missionary I had met in Trinidad a week earlier. What a relief to know I was safe. That experience, and many more like it that summer, taught me that I could trust God to protect and deliver me.

More recently, my wife and I went on a trip that involved a number of stops in an Asian country. One night we were being taken to the airport at about 3:00 a.m. When the driver got to a "T" in the road, he turned to us and asked, "Which way?"

Startled, since we were total strangers to the city, I just said, "Airport."

He turned left and then over the next hour made all kinds of turns through deserted streets that to us were not at all familiar. At one point a couple of men walked out of an alley. When the driver stopped his car and got out I yelled to him, "Are you lost?"

He just turned and started walking briskly toward the two men. I didn't know if I should jump up to the front seat and drive away or wait and see. I turned to Mur and said, "I guess it's time to pray," which we did.

Shortly he returned, got in the car and said quietly, "Airport, just around the corner about one kilometer."

We were relieved when after turning the corner we could see the airport. God had protected us.

From there we flew into a remote state of the country that was experiencing some terrorist activity. In fact, the terrorists had called an all day strike. While flying to our destination the pilot talked to Mur twice asking, "Where are you planning to get off?"

When Mur gave our destination, he said, "Are you sure?" It was clear he didn't think it would be wise for us to do that. After we landed, however, our friend from the city there met us and helped us through customs.

On our way to the city where we would be leading a pastors' conference we were stopped by the military. Our friend had the right papers and a position of influence so they let us through. We arrived in the evening.

Because of the strike, many of the participants couldn't make it to the conference site, so, they cancelled the first day. Every morning we were awakened by the sound of soldiers marching past the house where we stayed. They were heavily armed and followed by armed vehicles. During our time there they killed about 40 terrorists and took many more captive.

When we left for the airport after the conference soldiers lined the streets of the village on both sides and then spaced themselves farther apart all along the highway. As we passed, many of them smiled and waved. When we got to the airport, while I was involved in checking in, the government agents in charge of security talked to Mur. They said to her, "We have to get you out of here alive or it will be more than a local problem. It will be an international incident."

We were the only foreigners in that state at the time, and they were concerned about our safety. God was looking out for us and used the authorities and soldiers to protect us. We were grateful, especially when we were high up in the air on our way to the capital, and then on home.

The Bible is replete with illustrations of the tension between God and His people and the devil and his minions. It is exciting to read how God both protects and delivers His own. They are not always delivered without a battle and battle scars, but God sees to it that His plan and purpose is realized. At times God wants us to simply stand still and trust Him to act. At other times He calls us to arm ourselves and engage in the battle. That is why Paul tells us in Ephesians 6:10-18 that God provides both defensive and offensive weapons for spiritual warfare. But even when we engage in the battle, it is won not by our might or power, but by His Spirit. Never forget this.

Application questions:
1. Can you remember a time when God protected you?
2. In what ways has that experience impacted your life?
3. When faced with danger how do you re-enforce your faith to prepare yourself to overcome the danger? ˙
4. Have you ever been trapped with no apparent way out, yet you experienced God delivering you?

Suggested Prayer:
"Almighty God, I feel trapped and in danger. Please send Your guardian angel to protect me and deliver me. Be my strength. Empower me to resist the enemy and overcome my fear. As I overcome I will praise You and give You all the glory. In the name of Jesus, Amen."

Chapter Nine

Our Calling:
Are You Really Calling Me,
God?

"One night...the Lord called Samuel." (1 Samuel 3:2-4)

Were you ever awakened from sleep a number of times by a recurring dream? Samuel was. He was living away from his home in the temple of God under the care of Eli, the high priest.

His mother Hanna had been childless. Year after year she waited to become pregnant. Finally, in desperation, she sought God in the temple. Her agony was so intense that she made God an offer. She promised God that if He would give her a son, she would give him back to the Lord for all the days of his life.

Eli noticed Hanna in her grief, and thought she was drunk. When he rebuked her she explained to him her agony of heart. After he heard her story he said to her,

"Go in peace, and may the God of Israel grant you what you have asked of him." (1 Samuel 1:17)

God did what Eli promised, and after Samuel was weaned from his mother she brought him to the temple and dedicated him to the Lord.

One night as young Samuel was sleeping he heard someone call him, *"Samuel!"*

He woke up and answered, *"Here I am."* When he didn't see someone standing there, he got up and ran to the bedroom of Eli the priest and said, *"Here I am: You called me."*

Stirred from his sleep all Eli could conclude was that young Samuel was dreaming something. He told him as graciously as he could to go back to sleep.

The call came again, *"Samuel!"*

He got up as before and went into Eli and said, *"Here I am: You called me."*

"My son," Eli said, *"I did not call; go back and lie down."*

At this point in the account of this night in 1 Samuel 3:7 it says, *"Now Samuel did not yet know the Lord: The word of the Lord had not yet been revealed to him."* We learn from this that even if you don't know the Lord or His Word, you still can hear His call. Responding to the call is an important step in receiving light in the night (or at any time) for living in the day.

When Samuel was called a third time, he got up, went to Eli and said, *"Here I am: You called for me."*

Eli finally realized that the Lord was calling the boy. So he said to Samuel, *"Go and lie down, and if he calls you, say, 'Speak Lord, for your servant is listening.'"* Samuel did as he was told.

The Lord came to Samuel and stood there, calling him as before, *"Samuel! Samuel!"*

This time Samuel answered as Eli instructed him: *"Speak, for your servant is listening."*

For the first time in his life Samuel received a word from God. God shared with him a very heavy message of judgment that He was planning to implement on the family of Eli: He *"...would judge Eli's family forever because of the sin he knew about; his sons made themselves contemptible, and he failed to restrain them."* (1 Samuel 3:13)

This guilt would never be able to be atoned for by any sacrifice or offering.

Samuel was so overwhelmed that he was reticent to share it with Eli the next morning. When Eli asked him what God had said, he was still not sure if he should tell him. Finally, Eli persuaded him to share the tragic news that would involve Eli and his sons as well as the whole nation.

Sometimes God calls individuals into a lifetime of ministry. At other times He calls people to do some specific task. When we hear His call, Samuel's response would always be acceptable to God, "Speak, for your servant is listening."

While having lunch one day with a good friend, Jim Surace, he shared how God gave him a unique call. He owned an insurance agency with about 30 agents and things were going well, but he was restless.

After becoming a believer in Jesus he found great joy in sharing his new life. With a passion for young people he served as a youth pastor for a number of years, while continuing in business. By February 2006 he was financially in a position to retire from business and spend the rest of his life doing full time ministry. In addition, as a successful businessman, he was asked to serve on the boards of a number of Christian ministries.

His restlessness, however, continued. Increasingly he felt a tug to turn the business over to someone else so he could devote more time to ministry. He brought a young friend, Marcus, into the business as a partner. He planned to mentor him for a year, then with the business going well, turn the managing of the agency over to him so he would be free to pursue ministry. Before making the transition Jim and his wife Nancy went on a trip to pray, discuss, think through, and finalize his plans. Upon returning he intended to implement the plan.

On the first night of the trip he had a dream. At first he thought he was running a sales training session with his agents. Then he related to me, "I noticed there were about 3 to 4 times as many people in my dream as we currently had in our agency and all of them seemed young, college age, very enthusiastic. The additional people from Toledo and Columbus were not, at that time, in our allowable agency geography. Gradually I realized I was not teaching insurance or sales as usual but rather I was teaching the Gospel of Jesus Christ. Unlike many of my past youth group experiences, all were listening intently to what I was saying and it seemed to have immediate impact."

When Jim awoke he sensed the dream was from the Lord so he pondered its meaning. After prayerful meditation he concluded the Lord was impressing three truths on his heart. Enthusiastically he shared them with me.

"The first and most emphatic truth was, *your business is your ministry.* Secondly, God said, *'I am going to bring your youth group to you.'* This was significant for a couple of reasons. It touched my heart since I was a youth minister for over 10 years and I always had a special love for young people. I worked hard trying to reach teenagers."

He continued, "As exciting as this was to me I began to question God, 'God, if I am to stay in business, I will need to invest and build. It seems a waste of time and money to me since I believe Jesus is coming back real soon. Wouldn't my time and money be better spent...' Before I could go on, God interrupted me with a question, *'What is it to you when I come back?'*"

"Well, that was all I needed to understand," he said with a confident glint in his eye. "This was the answer to my prayer,

'What we should do?' I told my wife Nancy the dream and the conclusion I had come to, that we would stay with the insurance agency and be obedient to the Lord."

Joy was written all over his face as he pointed out the results of his decision. "Now, almost two years later, we have grown to 120 people, most of them college age. These now would be the age of the teenagers I had ministered to and tried to reach when I was involved in youth ministry. It was like God was bringing my youth group back (like He said)…only a little older and a lot more. They are a very passionate, teachable, open group of young people. Many of their lives have been changed since coming with our agency. Many have given their lives to Jesus. Others have decided to be recommitted. We expect and anticipate miracles and changes in everyone the Lord leads to our company. We currently hold our meetings in the Ball Rooms of hotels because we are too large for our Office Building. The Toledo and Columbus Regions are now in our organization with offices opened up in both territories. These outcomes were both in the dream."

With a smile he went on, "In addition I have.had several opportunities to witness and talk about Jesus to top officials of the company I represent. I was asked to come and visit last year with our CEO relative to spiritual issues he was having. He is a non practicing Jew. I spent 4 hours at his house in Dallas going over the Bible. I am asked to pray with the CEO, CMO and other company officials before all of our national meetings. I've also been asked to speak at our national meetings where I've shared my faith in this business setting. I was chosen as SGA of 2006. In addition, God has enabled me to witness to many other Agency owners around the country."

In conclusion he declared, "Everything that was in the dream has come true." Truly, he was called by God to make his business his ministry for God. Once he grasped this and obeyed God's call God blessed him beyond his fondest hopes.

As a young couple, Bill and Vonette Bright, founders of Campus Crusade for Christ, were pursuing their dreams. After two years of living at a rather hectic pace they came to realize something had to change. They decided independently to write out their expectations in life and in their marriage. After discussing this further with each other, they wrote out and signed a contract with God to become "slaves," as Paul described himself in Romans 1:1. They didn't know what that would look like for them in the days ahead, but they didn't have to wait long for God to clarify His plan.

The next day, Bill, a student at Fuller Seminary, was studying with a friend late at night in preparation for a Hebrew exam. Unexpectedly he became aware of God's presence in a new way. "I can't explain it," he recalls, "except to say that I was enveloped in God's presence. What was most on His heart was suddenly imparted to mine: to seek and save the lost."

He didn't hear a voice from God or see anything physical, but he did receive a vision of the good news of Jesus Christ being taken to the world. He envisioned every person in the world having the opportunity to hear about Jesus Christ and know Him, starting with reaching future leaders on college campuses.

When he shared his experience with Dr. Wilbur Smith, one of his mentors at the seminary, his call was affirmed. After mulling over what Bill had experienced, Dr. Smith said repeatedly, "This is of God." He also was the one who came up with the name for Bill's mission: Campus Crusade for Christ.

Too often we've only emphasized the need for a "call" for those going into ministry. I believe we should all have a sense that what we are doing with our lives is in keeping with what God planned for us. And then there are times when we sense a "call" to do something special for a season, no matter how short or long that might be.

In re-reading the book by Brother Andrew, *God's Smuggler*, I was impressed with the many times God spoke to him during the night. One night, after attending a Christian meeting with a number of soldiers recovering from wounds suffered during war, he stumbled through a simple prayer, repeating words from a song sung at a meeting, "Let them go...let me go..." He hardly knew what he was saying, but after the night's sleep his life began to change.

Shortly after that, during a stormy night, he lay in his bed listening to the windblown sleet beat on the house. His imagination raced back to a number of events that came back to him. He could hear the voices of individuals who had shared with him tidbits of truth that now were coming together and tugging at his heart. Finally, he realized that his ego was standing between him and God. He had to let go of it. His prayer wasn't fancy or very long. Just, "Lord, if You will show me the way, I will follow You. Amen."

It was another nighttime experience when he responded to a call to become a missionary. And then, having been challenged by the girl he loved to be a missionary in his own community first, he determined to apply for a job at a large plant nearby. The night before he went to apply for the job he had a dream in which he saw workers at the plant come to him to find out what made his life so different. When he told them, they all got on their knees before God.

He soon found out that the real world in the plant was totally different from his dream. Instead of respect and receptiveness, he received ridicule. Things got worse before, eventually, he saw a ray of light. Then came a beam of light. Finally, he saw many of the workers come to faith in Jesus. His dream was fulfilled as he saw many of his co-workers take the step of putting their faith in Jesus Christ for salvation.

There are those who believe you should only go into full-time ministry if God gives you a very specific "call." They encourage people to stay out of ministry if they can. I question how that corresponds to the revelation God has given in His Word. He commands all of us to take up the responsibility to let our lights shine, so the watching world will see what God can do in and through a life that is surrendered fully to Him (Matthew 5:16).

God also told the church to take the gospel message to the whole world, to all peoples. He told the apostles to take the gospel message first to Jerusalem, then to Judea and Samaria, and then to the ends of the world (Acts 1:8). They, however, stayed in Jerusalem until God allowed persecution to drive believers out into surrounding territories and beyond. Lay people led the way. Acts 8:1-4 says,

> *"On that day a great persecution broke out against the church at Jerusalem, and all except the apostles were scattered throughout Judea and Samaria...Those who had been scattered preached the word wherever they went."*

Adrian Rogers was a Baptist pastor for more than 50 years. God blessed his ministry in his church so much that it spilled over into a radio and writing ministry that spanned the globe. While still in his teens he felt God calling him into the ministry, and he gladly surrendered to the call.

The burden he had to be used by God was so great he went out one night to the football field of the high school he was attending and started to pray for God's blessing. He wanted to humble himself so he got down on his knees. Still struggling, he then prostrated himself on the ground. Finally, he scraped out a small hole so that he could put his nose down into it. He couldn't put himself down any farther. There, all alone with God, he cried out to God, "Lord, I am as low as I know how to get. I want You to use me."

Nothing overt happened that night, but in his heart he sensed God had touched him in a special way. He believes God filled him with the Holy Spirit that night. And when that happened he began to see God using him in powerful ways. He testifies that his humble surrender that night began a journey of surrender. He was convinced that if God ever took His hand of blessing and power off his life he would be nothing.

My own experience of sensing the call of God was not dramatic. When I went to work in an office after graduating from high school, I wanted to let my light shine for God among my fellow workers. While working hard at doing a good job in the accounting department, I looked for opportunities to share the good news. I found, however, that I was not as prepared as I needed to be to buy up opportunities that came my way. After a year I decided to go to a Bible school where I could become better prepared to represent my Lord in the marketplace. I fully intended to return to the kind of work I was doing at the time.

While in Bible school it was required of students to be involved in outreach efforts. It was not an option. So, I prepared to do the best I could. To my amazement, people would say that they were helped by what I shared with them. The summer after my first year of school I went on an outreach trip to Jamaica. My decision to go was based on the clear teaching in the Bible that we are to get the message out. All I was doing was obeying and buying up an opportunity that opened before me.

When I got to Jamaica, however, another student I was planning to serve with had not arrived. Nor had he contacted me or the people with whom we were going to work. I was faced with a decision about whether I should stay there and do what I could by myself or buy up another opportunity to go to South America and help the YFC team in Caracas, Venezuela, prepare for a large youth congress. I flew to Jamaica with the Caribbean director of YFC and his associate, and they were on their way to Trinidad, just off the coast of Venezuela where the congress was going to take place.

As I sought the Lord, praying and reading the Bible, I came across this statement in Proverbs 20:24: *"A man's steps are directed by the Lord. How then can anyone understand his own way?"* Though I didn't understand all that was happening, my sense was that God wanted me to go on to South America. As I shared my decision with the folks in Jamaica, they, too, could not understand everything, but they affirmed my decision and sent me off with their blessing. This all took place the one night we were in Jamaica. It was light in the night for living in the day. My time enroute and the experiences in Venezuela that summer left an indelible impression on my life.

Gradually, over a period of time, while I continued my education and engaged in other outreach efforts at home and abroad, I became aware of God's hand upon me. He indeed gifted me to teach His Word. I spent much time during this process searching my heart and God's Word regarding the matter of serving God full time.

When I proposed to my wife, I told her that she would have to be willing to take third place in my life. God was first. Doing His work was second. She would be third. I hinted at this prior to proposing, and she was not certain I meant what I said. But to be certain she would not be swept off her feet, she prepared a list of 20 reasons why she would not accept my proposal. Fortunately for me, she forgot them the night I proposed, and she agreed to become my wife.

Her commitment was tested early in our marriage. Within months I went on a mission trip during our first Christmas. When I returned it was obvious to me that she was deeply hurt by my decision to go on that trip and leave her alone at home, especially since she was having a rough time early in her first pregnancy. She communicated her hurt by being very cool to me when I returned home.

I remember sleepless nights wrestling over the reality that if our marriage was going to crumble because of my idealistic priorities I would disqualify myself for ministry. God made it clear to me during those sleepless nights that my conviction that He demands first place in my life was correct. However, I came to see that all other relationships, responsibilities and commitments must constantly be managed under His oversight. In other words, if my wife had a special need, that would take preference over my work for God. At other times a pressing need in my work for God might take precedent over some planned activity with my wife. And when we had children, their needs were at times as important or more important than other commitments. There needed to be a dynamic moment by moment awareness of what God wanted as a priority for me.

This light, which emerged during those trying nights of struggle, aided me in making responsible decisions as a husband, father, servant of God and as a man regarding my own personal needs. Maintaining this balance under God's supervision is what I refer to in the title of my book, A *Call to Responsible Freedom*.

At the time I believed I would be going into an itinerant Bible teaching ministry where I would be traveling most of the time. But while still in college an opportunity opened for me to pastor a small Bible Church. I thought this would provide good experience for me in preparing and delivering messages, so I accepted the offer. That became the beginning of pastoral ministry that has lasted over forty five years in four churches. Each of the churches has given me the privilege of traveling a fair amount to teach, preach and encourage Christian leaders all over the world. And now through writing and a daily radio ministry I see that what I felt God was leading me into is being fulfilled in ways I would never have dreamed possible.

Like the Word of God, which *"...is a lamp to my feet and a light for my path"* (Psalm 119:105), God has given me light, often at night, for fulfilling His call on my life.

God's call is very distinct for some and comes over them unexpectedly. Others take steps of deeper commitment gradually, and in the process sense God impressing His call on them incrementally. There are times when God's call is for a specific task and time. In my case I became aware of God's call with hindsight. Gradually, I became convinced He had called and gifted me for what I was doing. It is important to be open and ready to respond when the call comes.

Application Questions:
1. Have you ever sensed the call of God to do something you would otherwise not have considered doing?
2. Was the call for a short time task or was it for a lifetime commitment?
3. How did you respond to that call and what was the outcome?
4. If you have not sensed the call of God on your life what are your thoughts regarding the fact that God has called the church to take the gospel to the world? What is your contribution or responsibility to that mission?

Suggested Prayer:
"Loving heavenly Father, I know that You love sinners so much that You sent Your only Son, Jesus Christ, to become their Savior. You also commissioned Your church to reach out to the world with this Good News in the power of the Holy Spirit. Help me to discern Your will for me in that great mission and help me to surrender to Your will. I want to do all You have purposed for me. In Jesus' name, Amen."

Lud Golz

Chapter Ten

Provision: When Are You Going to Come Through, God?

"The Lord your God has been with you, and you have not lacked anything." (Deuteronomy 2:7)

As I shared in a previous chapter, Mur and I were in a quandary when I resigned from my pastoral position 31 years ago. I didn't have peace about pursuing two opportunities for work that were offered to me. Life, however, does not stop and wait for us. During those days and nights Mur prayed the words of a song she had learned as a child in Sunday school.

"He owns the cattle on a thousand hills, the wealth in every mine;
He owns the rivers and the rocks and rills, the sun and stars that shine.
Wonderful riches, more than tongue can tell –
He is my Father so they're mine as well;
He owns the cattle on a thousand hills –
I know that He will care for me."

This song was an encouragement to trust God to go before us and open the door He wanted us to go through. It also encouraged us to believe God would provide all that we needed.

Since nothing was opening up, Mur and I decided to do some house searching. There was less than five weeks' time left for us to live in the parsonage. School was starting for our children within days. With no equity in a house, since we had always lived in a parsonage, our options were limited. Our savings were minimal. The only equity we had was in some property we had purchased in the past in a couple of recreational developments. Nevertheless, we felt as though God was directing us to look into purchasing a home in the area so the children would not have to change schools.

After a long day of looking at homes with a realtor, we thought we would go out for a short drive after dinner. As we drove down a street near us, we noticed a "For Sale" sign in front of a house right where we often thought was a desirable location. The property overlooked one thousand acres of undeveloped woods and rolling hills except for a beautiful headquarters complex of an international organization. To our surprise the house was being sold through our realtor's company.

When we got home, we called her and asked why she hadn't shown us this house. She said, "I thought it was too small."

We told her, "We're very interested in looking at it. Could you set up an appointment for tomorrow?"

"I'll try."

Later that night she called the owners. When she asked about setting up an appointment the wife responded, "Didn't you get the message I left at the realty office?"

She hadn't.

The owner called the realty office that afternoon and told them, "Please don't set up any more visits." She quietly thought for a moment and then said, "OK. I have a good feeling about this." The appointment was set up for the next morning.

After walking through the house we sensed that this was the house for us. The realtor was surprised when we said, "We like this. When can you work up a contract to sign?"

"Don't you want to talk it over together?"

We said, "We told you that we were interested in it, and we sense that we should just go ahead."

After we drove to the parsonage she wrote up a contract. In the contract we stipulated we would put 20% down and establish a twenty year mortgage, subject to obtaining financing. That was because we didn't have the 20% to put down, and our qualifications for getting a mortgage without having a job didn't look very promising.

After working through a few counter-proposals with the owners, we signed a contract on the Saturday of Labor Day weekend. The next day a new church start, made up of people we knew from our former church, was having its first meeting – just three weeks after I had resigned. The congregation had asked me if I would speak. Since I was not committed elsewhere, I agreed.

More than 100 people attended that first meeting in a local town hall. After the service leaders of the group again asked me if I would consider becoming their pastor. Since I needed work, and since we had signed a contract for a home, and since school was starting for our children that week, I decided to accept their offer. Though we had agonized in prayer, day and night, it seemed to us to be a rather obvious, pragmatic decision.

Among those in that first meeting was a couple in our community whose son had died the week after I resigned. They came to us for help and to do the memorial service for their son. This resulted in a relationship between us that serendipitously helped us a couple of weeks later. He was a banker.

When I asked Reggie Brooks if he could help us with getting a mortgage, he said he couldn't do it himself because his bank was in another county, but he would set up an appointment with a friend of his who was an officer in a local bank. We went with him to that appointment the day after Labor Day.

Judy Taylor greeted us warmly, and after introductions she opened her pad to take down some information. She began by asking questions. "Where do you live?"

"In a parsonage," I replied.

"Where do you work?"

"At a new church."

"How long have you served there?"

"Two days."

"How long has the church existed?"

"Two days."

"What is the name of the church?"

"We don't have a name yet."

Incredulous, Judy closed the pad. Reggie smiled and said to her, "I know many of the people who are starting this new church, and I vouch for their credibility. Why don't we go out for lunch together?" Relieved, she agreed.

At the lunch she asked me to describe what I envisioned for the new church, and I shared as best I could what I would like to see happen. After lunch she said she would get back to us.

Later that week I played golf with one of the men in our new church. After our round of golf he said to me as we drove home, "I don't know what your financial situation is, but I want you to know that I have about $17,000 in an investment that is paying me 7%. You can borrow any or all of it if you need to, at 7% interest, and we can do it on a handshake!"

At the time that was enough to cover a little more than the 20% down payment we had agreed to in our contract. This, to us, was obviously God's provision, and we accepted his offer so we could make the down payment.

Within a week we got a call from Judy letting us know that the mortgage would be available. All we had to do was come to her office and sign the contract.

What an amazing provision God made for us. The church decided to give us a housing allowance that covered the monthly mortgage payment. Nineteen years later our mortgage was paid in full. The house is now ours. No, it's His!

This whole sequence of events is to us as miraculous as what is recorded in 2 Kings 6 and 7. The story begins with the king of Aram being at war with Israel. Whenever he set up a plan of attack, Elisha would tell the king of Israel the enemy's plans and how the king could defend his nation. The king of Aram was infuriated and wanted to find who was leaking information about his plans to the Israelites. When he summoned his officers, one of them told him that it was the prophet Elisha. When they tracked down where Elisha was living, they encircled his house. Elisha prayed that they would be blinded. God answered. Then he led the blinded army right into the city of Samaria. He prayed again that their eyes would be opened. When God opened their eyes they were surprised to see they were surrounded by the king of Israel and his army.

When the king asked Elisha if he should kill them, he instructed him, *"Do not kill them...Would you kill men you have captured with your own sword or bow? Set food and water before them so that they may eat and drink and then go back to their master."*

The king did what Elisha had instructed him to do.

"Some time later, Ben-Hadad king of Aram mobilized his entire army, marched up and laid siege to Samaria. There was a great famine in the city" because of the siege. It was so bad that

people resorted to eating their own children to survive. The King of Israel remembered that it was Elisha who had instructed him not to kill the army of Aram and now they were ready to be strangled by them. He went to Elisha ready to kill him, but Elisha told him that the very next day the strangle hold would be over and they would have plenty of food for everyone.

The king's officer derided Elisha, saying, *"Look, even if the Lord should open the floodgates of the heavens, could this happen?"* Elisha responded, *"You will see it with your own eyes, but you will not eat any of it."*

There were four lepers at the city gate. They convinced each other that their best option was to go to the enemy troops surrounding the city and surrender. So at dusk they went to the camp of the Arameans. Ready to surrender, they were surprised to find the camp abandoned. 2 Kings 7:6-7 says,

> *"The Lord had caused the Arameans to hear the sound of chariots and horses and a great army, so that they said to one another, 'Look, the king of Israel has hired the Hittite and Egyptian kings to attack us!' So they got up and fled in the dusk and abandoned their tents and their horses and donkeys. They left the camp as it was and ran for their lives."*

The lepers were delirious with the sight. They gorged themselves and started hiding some of the loot. Verse 9 says, *"Then they said to each other, 'We're not doing right. This is a day of good news and we are keeping it to ourselves. If we wait until daylight, punishment will overtake us. Let's go at once and report this to the royal palace.'"*

When they did this, the first response of the king was to suspect a plot to ambush anyone who would leave the city. An officer suggested that a contingent of soldiers should be sent to check out the story and see if, indeed, the army of Aram had left. When they found it to be as reported, what remained in the camp of the enemy was more than sufficient to provide for everyone in the city. In fact, the rush to get to the food and loot was so great that they trampled under foot the officer who had questioned God's ability to do what Elisha had predicted. This deliverance, which resulted in God's bountiful provision, took place at night and, thus, was another time when God gave light in the night for living in the day.

Reflecting on the theme of God's provision, there appears to be a tendency on God's part to wait until we are in an extreme position before He comes through and provides what we need. But we forget that most of the time He is providing what we need without our even asking Him. We remember the former because we are so conscious of our need, and then, of God's provision. Possibly, if we were more grateful for His ongoing provision of daily necessities we would avoid some of the things that get us into the more trying circumstances. It's good to remember Paul's affirmation in 2 Timothy 2:13 (KJV),

"If we believe not, yet he abideth faithful: he cannot deny himself."

Application Questions:
1. Can you recall a time when God provided just what you needed at the critical moment?
2. As you were faced with the critical moment approaching did you have confidence that God would provide? If you did, what do you believe gave you that confidence?
3. Have you had the opportunity to encourage someone in need by sharing how God provided for you?

4. Has God used you to provide help for someone else in need?

5. How have these experiences impacted your prayer life?

Suggested Prayer:

"Heavenly Father, You have encouraged me to come to You in time of need and ask for Your provision. Thank You for this invitation and for the many promises You have given that You will provide, even way above what we ask or think. I thank You for the times You have provided in the past. I come again, asking that You would meet my present need. And I thank You in advance for granting my request. In Jesus' name, Amen."

Chapter Eleven

Disciplines for Receiving Light in the Night: What Do I Do Now?

"On my bed I remember you; I think of you through the watches of the night." (Psalm 63:6)

I have been sharing how God often speaks to people or works some of His mighty works in the night. These communiqués or actions are designed to give light in the night for living in the day. This doesn't mean God cannot and does not communicate to us or act in our behalf during the day. He often has in the past, and I'm sure He will in the future. But what I wanted to emphasize is that there are times we might miss His communiqué or intended action if we are not tuned in to recognizing it and responding appropriately to receiving the desired outcome.

The psalmist wanted the intimacy of his relationship with God to be as real in the middle of the night as it was in the day. When he woke up during the night, instead of being frustrated and restless, he tried to remember the Lord. He would think of Him through the night watches (Psalm 63:6 and 119:148). But how do you do this? What are the disciplines necessary to receive whatever light God might want to give us even in the night?

Lovers always want to know that their sweethearts are thinking about them, 24/7. That's not practically possible, but whenever it is possible, true love craves that. A phone call, a whisper in the ear, a love note, doing something special to remind, listening intently, embracing; these and many other expressions telegraph clearly a person is thinking about the one he or she loves. I believe God desires the same from His own. Frankly, I believe He craves that. If you have a healthy relationship with Him, you will crave the same from Him. What this does is set the stage for receiving His expressions of love and light at any time, including during the night watches.

In an August 14, 2006 NEWSWEEK article Jon Meacham writes how Billy Graham shared with him a night time experience. When he awoke during the night he began reciting the 23rd Psalm from memory: *"The Lord is my shepherd, I shall not want..."* Struggling to continue he found his mind blank. Then he remembered the closing words of the Psalm: *"Surely thy loving-kindness and mercy shall follow me all the days of my life; and I will dwell in the house of the Lord forever."* Comforted by this promise he drifted back to sleep.

What was interesting to me was not that he forgot some of the well known Psalm. The important thing to me was that when he awoke his thoughts immediately went to God's Word. And though he didn't remember all of Psalm 23, what he remembered comforted him.

Later in the article Meacham writes how Billy Graham recalled an incident early in his evangelistic career when he was challenged by a friend about whether the Bible was the inerrant Word of God. While wrestling over this issue in his mind he went out one night into the woods at the conference grounds, opened his Bible and set it on a tree stump. Turning to God he prayed honestly that he didn't know all that was in the Bible and wasn't always able to explain it adequately, but he was going to believe that it is God's divine Word. Since then it has shaped his life and ministry.

One way the psalmist prepared himself for such experiences is described in Psalm 1:1-3: *"Blessed is the man who does not walk in the counsel of the wicked or stand in the way of sinners or sit in the seat of mockers. But his delight is in the law of the Lord, and on his law he meditates day and night. He is like a tree planted by streams of water, which yields its fruit in season and whose leaf does not wither. Whatever he does prospers."*

There are two word pictures presented in these verses. The first is a picture of someone seeking counsel or input for making decisions in life. If you want your life blessed, the psalmist says you need to be careful from whom you get your counsel. The wicked, sinners or mockers represent a worldly perspective on life. Don't seek that counsel. In fact, don't even associate with those who have that perspective. Be aware that you can be misled even by the wrong kind of friends. Get your counsel from God by meditating on His Word day and night.

The second picture describes the life of one who.gets counsel from God's Word. They will be like a fruitful, beautiful tree that is growing by streams of water. I grew up in western Canada where you have the Rocky Mountains. As you look at these towering mountains you notice that there is what is called a tree line. Beyond that line you do not see any big trees. The further you go down the mountain the trees become larger. It's in the valleys that you find the largest trees, usually growing close to streams or rivers.

Most of us like mountain top experiences. The view is breathtaking. The air is fresh. It is exhilarating. But you don't find growth taking place there. Growth takes place in the valleys. It is similar in the Christian life. There is nothing wrong with spiritual mountain top experiences. God often sets them up for us to enjoy.

But we need to realize that generally growth doesn't result from those experiences. Most of life is lived in the valleys. The dark, damp places we often try to avoid. When you are there, and you open God's Word and reflect upon it, you will find that most of God's Word applies to those kinds of settings. And many of the experiences of Bible characters also take place in the valleys, often in the night.

The discipline described here involves being familiar enough with God's Word that you are able to meditate on it wherever you are, whenever you want to. One of the saddest realities in the church today is that we are becoming more and more biblically illiterate. Few of us work at mastering the Word of God, let alone memorize it. Why? Could it be that we have not feasted on it sufficiently to delight in it? Many find it boring or irrelevant. If you are not able to remember what it says, you will have a hard time meditating on it, as the psalmist did, day and night. If you don't meditate on it, you won't discover its implications and relevance to your life.

I believe that without mastering and memorizing God's Word in the day, you will not be able to meditate on it in the night. If you have memorized a verse or paragraph or chapter in the Bible, there is a good possibility that your mind will be reviewing it subconsciously while you sleep. This would especially be true if you reviewed a portion of the Bible before you went to sleep. Again, it is easier to do if you have memorized God's Word.

In addition, if you awake from your sleep, you can take a moment to review what you reflected on before you went to sleep. Think about what it says. Ask yourself if there is something in what you have reviewed that might help you in anything you are facing at the time. If nothing else, use what you are meditating on to draw closer to God. Let it be a springboard for prayer and praise.

During my first year in Bible school I memorized the book of Ephesians. While on an overnight bus trip from St. Petersburg, Florida to Miami, I spent the long hours praying. I would review a section of Ephesians and then pray using the thoughts I had meditated on. It was a most refreshing experience. I didn't need to bother anyone by having my reading light on. And the time went by a lot faster. I have found throughout the years that using scripture in my praying has strengthened my faith and clarified what I should be praying.

Prayer is the next discipline it would be good to work on. Prayer is just talking to God. The more intimate your relationship with anyone, the more you will want to communicate with each other. You will want to share ideas, impressions, questions, joys, sorrows, dreams. I believe that is true in any intimate relationship, but it is especially true in your relationship with God. He wants to hear what is on your heart. He already knows before you share, but He takes delight in hearing you express your concerns or delights.

It's in that intimate relationship that He also wants to share His concerns, delights or designs with you. These . often will become light in the night for living in the day. You might be able to be used by Him to address and share His concerns with others. His concerns let you know that He loves you and cares about your welfare. His delights will give you the sense that He is with you and will go before you. His designs give you a sense of direction and call.

When you intercede for others, what you are doing is broadening the impact of God in and through them. Remember Esther. When she called for a three day fast, day and night, it not only opened the door for her to see God at work in her life, but it also gave those who joined her, a sense of being used by God. In addition it involved the king and his actions. That prepared the way for Mordecai to be honored and for the nation of Israel to be protected from extinction.

Thanksgiving and praise in prayer takes this all a step further. It is an affirmation of your appreciation of what God has done in the past. It also affirms devotion to Him for Who He is. And it is an affirmation that you are confident what He has done in the past, He will do in the future because of Who He is. All of this contributes to our intimacy with God and encourages a greater degree of expectation for the future.

I don't know if Paul had a good voice or not, but he joined his partner Silas in song one night. They had been beaten and thrown into a rat-infested prison with their feet in stocks. Bleeding and in pain, they finally began praying and singing hymns at midnight (Acts 16:25). To many this might seem incredulous. To them it was natural. Their prayers and songs not only lifted their spirits, they touched the heart of God. He responded by sending an earthquake that ultimately set them free. But probably even more important, it opened the door for the jailer and his family to be set free through their prayer for salvation. It became a significant part of planting a church in the city of Philippi that had far-reaching effects that are still felt today.

Music is something that emotionally captures all we have been thinking about. Those who have written psalms and hymns and spiritual songs have given expression of their heart cry either in petition or praise. It is a way of affirming and then remembering and reaffirming something over again. It usually generates an interest in others catching what is going on and then joining in themselves.

In the book of Job, Elihu says, *"God my Maker...gives songs in the night."* The Psalmist says the same in Psalm 42:8, *"By day the Lord directs his love, at night his song is with me – a prayer to the God of my life."* Again in Psalm 77:6, *"I remembered my songs in the night. "* And in Psalm 149:5, *"Let the saints rejoice in this honor and sing for joy on their beds. "* When you either write songs or learn songs that others have written, you will be prepared for those special times when they will be a great help in time of need.

I remember reading about an unusual experience on the World War 1 battlefield one Christmas eve. There was a lull in the fighting. One German soldier started singing a Christmas carol. Soon others joined in. Suddenly they heard a voice from across the no man zone singing a carol in English. Others joined in. It was a remarkable moment when the words of the carol, "Peace on earth, good will toward men," were momentarily fulfilled. Songs truly are powerful.

It was on another Christmas Eve, during the Civil War, that Henry Wadsworth Longfellow wrote a poem, just six months after the Battle of Gettysburg. Nine years later it was put to music. Over the years it has brought hope to many caught in the grip of despair.

> *"I heard the bells on Christmas day their old familiar carols play,*
> *And wild and sweet the words repeat of peace on earth, good will to men.*
> *And in despair I bowed my head: 'there is no peace on earth,' I said,*
> *'For hate is strong, and mocks the song of peace on earth, good will to men.'*
> *Yet pealed the bells more loud and deep:*
> *'God is not dead, nor doth He sleep;*
> *The wrong shall fail, the right prevail, with peace on earth, good will to men.'*
> *Then ringing, singing on its way, the world revolved from night to day –*
> *A voice, a chime, a chant sublime of peace on earth, good will to men. "*

There is something, however, that will hinder you from recognizing the light God wants to give you, an unforgiving heart. We need to confess our sins to God if we want to experience His forgiveness and love (1 John 1:9). But if we have an unforgiving heart toward someone else, we will become spiritually blind and insensitive.

As I shared earlier, I went through a valley of pain a number of years ago. I felt forced to resign from my pastorate because of false rumors that especially one man was spreading. After I resigned I became pastor of the church I have now been with for 31 years. At first I attempted to see if some of the barriers could be resolved with my former church. Every attempt backfired. Then one night I read what Paul said in Romans 12:18-21:

> *"If it is possible, as far as it depends on you, live at peace with everyone... 'If your enemy is hungry, feed him; if he is thirsty, give him something to drink. In doing this, you will heap burning coals on his head.' Do not be overcome by evil, but overcome evil with good."*

If you take verse 18 and read the three phrases backward it helps to understand the application God wants you to make. The objective in all of our relationships is to *"live at peace with everyone."* You might say that is impossible. All of us have relationships with irregular people. That's a nice way of saying, "People who rub you the wrong way or who have hurt you deeply."

How do you live at peace with such people? Start by considering the next phrase, *"as far as it depends on you."* That is, ask yourself, "What steps can I take to live at peace with them." This doesn't say we should force a superficial peace in our relationship. That would break down under pressure. Rather, we should do all we can to minimize anything that would trigger stress or conflict in the relationship. We should ask God for wisdom to do things that would make things go well in the relationship. Yes, it might even involve keeping our distance. Our very presence might stir up animosity.

Why do I suggest these possibilities as ways to *"live at peace with everyone,"* including those irregular people? Because Paul suggests in the opening phrase that doing any more than that is not possible. He says, *"If it is possible."* I've concluded that with some people it is best for me not to push a relationship. If I've had a relationship with them I might need to "cool it." If I can't help but spend time with them due to the circumstances, then I need to be cordial and gracious, and forgiving if necessary.

This might sound like I consider them to be enemies. No, mature love operates within the parameters of understanding. Philippians 1:9-10 says,

> *"And this is my prayer: that your love may abound more and more in knowledge and depth of insight, so that you may be able to discern what is best and may be pure and blameless until the day of Christ, filled with the fruit of righteousness that comes through Jesus Christ. to the glory and praise of God."*

The way love works is that even if your enemy is hungry, you feed him; if he is thirsty, you give him a drink. When it says, *"In doing this, you will heap burning coals on his head,"* I always interpreted it as being a way to get back at someone who has hurt me. That is, kill them with kindness. But Dr. Kenneth Wuest suggests a different perspective.

This was written in a culture where a necessity of life was having burning coals to provide heat for cooking and for keeping you warm. If your enemy has experienced such a setback that he doesn't even have coals to burn, then you should fill a bucket with burning coals and give it to him. In that culture they carried heavy objects on their heads. The point Paul is making is to help provide for them not only food and water but the necessary hot coals for cooking and comfort. Give them a heaping bucket of hot coals and let them keep the bucket. In this way you don't let evil overcome you, but you overcome evil with good.

That night while reflecting on these verses, I took a deliberate step of faith and commitment. I wanted any vestige of bitterness removed from my heart so it would not hinder God from working in my life and using me to further His kingdom. No one had contacted me asking for forgiveness, but I felt I needed to forgive everyone who had hurt me or contributed to my having to resign. I wanted God to know I was serious in my decision. I wanted to do more than just tell God I was willing to forgive.

As I prayed and reflected over this, a thought came to me. We live on a highway with a slight incline in the road in front of our property. For some reason a number of accidents took place directly in front of our home. When they occurred, we always invited those in the accident into our home, use our phone to call family or police, and offer them a cup of coffee.

In my prayer that night I felt as though I could 'nail down my promise to forgive by telling God, "As a token of my seriousness, Father, I promise you that if anyone who injured me has an accident in front of our home, I will treat him as graciously as I've treated others. That includes the person who deeply hurt me and my reputation. In that way I will demonstrate to You, God, that I have truly forgiven him."

That commitment became to me light in the night for living in the day.

To date God has never put me to the test on that commitment. But I can testify that from that night on I have been released from any bitterness and have had peace that my forgiveness was genuine, more than just words. I have been free, as Paul said in

Galatians 5:13, to serve others in love. It's been obvious that God subsequently has opened many doors for service that might not have come to me had I not taken the step of forgiveness that night.

As I am writing this chapter 31 years later, I am happy to report that recently I had the privilege of filling the pulpit of my former church while its present pastor was on vacation! In God's time He works things out to accomplish what is good and what will glorify Him.

I'm sure there are other disciplines God might use, but let me reiterate the basic disciplines I have suggested: hiding God's Word in your mind and heart, prayer, thanksgiving, songs of praise, confession of any known sin, and forgiveness. Making these disciplines a vital part of your life will open the door for you to experience what James 1:17 says,

> *"Every good and perfect gift is from above, coming down from the Father of the heavenly lights, who does not change like shifting shadows."*

Application Questions:
1. Of the disciplines mentioned in the chapter, which one is strongest in your life experience?
2. Which one of the disciplines mentioned in this chapter is weakest in your life experience?
3. What can you do to strengthen this discipline in your life?
4. Are there any other disciplines that you believe have helped you become better prepared to receive light from God?

Suggested Prayer:
"Dear heavenly Father, I want to be open and prepared to receive from You every good and perfect gift You want to give me. Help me to work on the disciplines that will better prepare me.

Then, when You do give me light, help me to be receptive and responsive so that Your purpose might be realized. Thank You for providing the many examples we have considered in this book to encourage me in this pursuit. In Jesus' name, Amen."

Chapter Twelve

A Final Word: Warning! What Happens If...?

"And God said, 'Let there be light'" (Genesis 1:3).

"Hear and pay attention, do not be arrogant, for the Lord has spoken. Give glory to the Lord your God before your feet stumble on the darkening hills. You hope for light, but he will turn it to thick darkness and change it to deep gloom." (Jeremiah 13:15-16)

We began this study by suggesting that our lives are so filled with activity, noise and distractions that God often chooses to share His light with us during the night. If we are responsive to the light God gives and integrate it into our lives God's purpose in giving the light will be fulfilled through us.

Jesus explained how this happens in His sermon on the mount:

"You are the light of the world. A city on a hill cannot be hidden. Neither do people light a lamp and put it under a bowl. Instead they put it on its stand, and it gives light to everyone in the house. In the same way, let your light

shine before men, that they may see your good deeds and praise your Father in heaven." (Matthew 5:14-16)

When we let our light shine openly before a watching world we will be what Daniel says in his prophecy,

"Those who are wise (or impart wisdom) will shine like the brightness of the heavens, and those who lead many to righteousness, like the stars for ever and ever." (Daniel 12:3)

But the reverse is also true. Scientists tell us that many bright shining stars are being drawn by the strong gravitational pull of black holes in our galaxies into their vortex and extinguished.

If we either keep the light to ourselves or resist the light given, a negative dynamic begins to take place. The light God wants you and the world around you to see and know experientially will be sucked into the black hole of the kingdom of darkness. I call this the spiritual law of the black hole.

Darkness is the absence of light. God, who is light, is in the business of providing light. Light dispels darkness. God doesn't want us to walk in darkness; confused, disoriented, directionless, in despair and without hope. We have seen in our study that God often gives to individuals and nations light in the night for living in the day.

There are many ways we can cultivate a sensitivity to the light He provides so that we benefit from it. But there are also ways we can resist and even turn off His light. Worse yet, God warns us that beyond a certain point of resistance or rebellion He might snuff out the light we need.

The prophet Micah warned of this, as did many other servants of God over the centuries. Because God's people were ignoring Him and worshiping idols God declared through Micah:

> *"Therefore night will come over you, without visions, and darkness without divination. The sun will set for the prophets, and the day will go dark for them. The seers will be ashamed and the diviners disgraced. They will all cover their faces because there is no answer from God."*
> (Micah 3:6-7)

Another prophet, Amos, warns God's people as well:

> *"'The days are coming,' declares the Sovereign Lord, 'when I will send a famine through the land – not a famine of food or a thirst for water, but a famine of hearing the words of the Lord. Men will stagger from sea to sea and wander from north to east, searching for the word of the Lord, but they will not find it.'"*
> (Amos 8:11-12)

These predictions by the prophets were fulfilled historically. For a period of four hundred years God provided no prophets, and there was no answer from Him to the desperate cries of His people. It was a period that could be described as the "dark ages" before Christ.

Then, in mercy and grace, God sent His Son into the darkness. John begins his Gospel by declaring that in Christ *"was life, and that life was the light of men."* (John 1:4) After describing to Nicodemus the provision of eternal life through His sacrifice on the cross Jesus warned,

"This is the verdict: Light has come into the world, but men loved darkness instead of light because their deeds were evil." (John 3:19)

God doesn't force His light on us. Later John says,

"Jesus spoke again to the people...I am the light of the world. Whoever follows me will never walk in darkness, but will have the light of life." (John 8:12)

A few chapters later He warns,

"Now is the time for judgment on this world...You are going to have the light just a little while longer. Walk while you have the light, before darkness overtakes you. The man who walks in the dark does not know where he is going. Put your trust in the light while you have it, so that you may become sons of light." (John 12:30-36)

Fortunately, there were a few who heeded His warning, came to the light and started walking in the light. And though the flicker of light seemed to be rather small it soon burst into a flame that spread throughout the world.

Centuries later the world again drifted into the dark ages. What before was the center of dynamic Christian light in Turkey and Greece became overwhelmed in spiritual darkness. There again was a famine of hearing the word of God. An answer from God was not heard, and in that part of the world is hardly heard to this day.

The Reformation in Western Europe began with a flicker of light here and there. Men like Wycliffe, Luther and Calvin kindled that flame and others helped bring it to a blazing fire that swept across country after country. This was followed by others like Wesley, Carry and Edwards. Only God knows the full impact of the church on society and the world during the past few centuries.

But again we stand at a place where the warning Jesus proclaimed to the church at Ephesus needs to be heeded.

> *"I know your deeds, your hard work and your perseverance. I know that you cannot tolerate wicked men, that you have tested those who claim to be apostles but are not, and have found them false. You have persevered and have endured hardships for my name, and have not grown weary. Yet I hold this against you: You have forsaken your first love. Remember the height from which you have fallen! Repent and do the things you did at first. If you do not repent, I will come to you and remove your lamp-stand from its place."* (Revelation 2:2-5)

This was a church that was committed to purity of life. They also were diligent to maintain purity of doctrine. But they were not as careful to maintain their loving devotion to Jesus Christ. In Christ's mind that was tantamount to forsaking their first love. And that required repentance and a return to *"the things you did at first."*

I have visited Ephesus a number of times. The architectural remains are breathtaking to behold. The tour guide described how on the main street going down to the spectacular façade of the library there were places where lampstands once stood to light the street. They are no longer there. And the light that the church once provided in that great city is also gone. In fact there are probably fewer true believers in Christ in the whole country of Turkey today than once lived in the city of Ephesus. The spiritual law of the black hole has operated in that country and many others.

We, too, must beware of the spiritual law of the black hole.

I believe God again wants to speak forth through the Church and through Christians, "Let there be light!" If we are sensitive to the light God gives, recognize and receive it, and then live in the light of it before a watching world, I believe we will see God open doors. Multitudes in the valley of decision will be brought to the Light of the world, Jesus Christ, and find eternal life through Him. May the cry of the song, *Shine, Jesus, Shine*, be our constant prayer. May the Father's glory fill our nation and our hearts be ablaze for Him. May the river of grace and mercy overflow its banks as God's word goes forth to provide the light we and the world so desperately need.

Application questions:
1. In what ways do you see the spiritual law of the black hole already operating in our nation and world?
2. Can you identify some "points of light" that are stemming the impact of the spiritual law of the black hole?
3. What steps can you take to become a "point of light"?

Suggested Prayer:
"Dear Father of light, thank You for sending Your Son, Jesus Christ, into the world to become the light of the world. Thank You for shining His light into my heart and mind so that I could become a 'son of light,' and be a citizen of the Kingdom of Light. Trim the light in my life so that it might shine brightly in this dark world. As the world looks at my life may they see the light of Christ so clearly shining through me that they would be drawn to Him. As more and more are drawn to the light, may the light become brighter and brighter. Yes, Lord, set this nation ablaze with Your light. May it shine to the far reaches of this world. In Christ's name, Amen."

Afterword

While gathering permissions from the works quoted in this book I came across a story I had to include.

The story of how Chosen Books got started is best told by John Sherrill, who had a surprising dream one night early in 1971.

I was awake. There had been no transition between sleep and being fully, startlingly awake. Quietly, so as not to disturb Tib [Elizabeth], I propped my pillow against the headboard of the bed and sat up. In the pre-dawn light I could just make out the bureau in the corner of the room.

The picture was in black and white. It was of a group of people--Len LeSourd was there, and Len's wife, Catherine Marshall, Tib and I and some others I could not identify. We were all studying a pile of books spread out on a conference table. A block of copy said that this group of people had worked together for years, writing and editing Christian articles. Now they had banded together to do the same with books.

The vision was over. I could not get back to sleep so I went downstairs and made coffee. . . . I was excited but was also stunned, full of fear and misgivings. I knew nothing at all about business, still less about book publishing; what did all this mean?

When Tib began to stir, I took coffee up and told her about the vision and asked her what she thought of starting a publishing house. To my astonishment Tib, who knew, if possible, less about business than I, said, "Why not! It would be an adventure."

So I took the plunge and spoke to Len LeSourd. I told him about the vision and asked if he and Catherine would consider joining us.

The next day Len called me at home with the news that he and Catherine were definitely interested.

"But," said Len, and then came the words that were such a threat to me, "we couldn't join you now, of course. We couldn't publish books and work at Guideposts at the same time. That creates a problem for you too. You'll have to talk to the Peales, won't you." It wasn't a question; it was a statement.

I put down the phone slowly, drawing in a long, long breath. The Peales?

I went straight to the phone and called Norman Vincent Peale. When we met, he told me, "If God is leading you into Christian books, I have a suggestion. You've heard me talk about the key to success in any undertaking. Six words: *Find a need and fill it.*"

"And I'll tell you the need that I see. When I look at some of the Christian books coming across my desk, I'm appalled. Sloppy writing, sloppy editing, sloppy manufacturing. Aim for quality, John. Strive for it. Hold out for it even though it costs you time and money.

"Take a year off. Take the risk of living without a salary. Find adventure. And hold onto quality."

So we plunged ahead. We even had a Power Verse, given to us as a special encouragement: "For we are his workmanship, created in Christ Jesus unto good works, which God hath before ordained that we should walk in them" (Eph. 2:10 KJV). Our job was simply to walk the path He had planned for us.

References

Philip Yancey, *Where is God When it Hurts* (Grand Rapids, Michigan: Zondervan, 1990, 1977), 134.

Charles Finney, *Revival of Religion*

Charles W. Colson, *Born Again* (Grand Rapids, Michigan: Chosen Books. Inc., 1976), 130.

Judy Douglass, Executive Editor, *Until Everyone Has Heard* (Campus Crusade for Christ, 100 Lake Hart Dr., Orlando, Florida, 2001), 13.

Brother Andrew and John and Elizabeth Sherrill, *God's Smuggler* (Uhricksville, Ohio: Barbour and Company, Inc., 1976), 36.

John Sherrill, *The History of Chosen Books* (from the "About Us" page on Chosen Books website).

For more information about other books by Lud Golz or the radio ministry of Lud Golz or to order copies of this book,
go to the following website:
www.gettinggodsmessage.org.

or send an email to

ludgolz@outlook.com.